READINGS ON

CYRANO DE BERGERAC

THE GREENHAVEN PRESS
Literary Companion
TO WORLD LITERATURE

READINGS ON

CYRANO DE BERGERAC

Crystal R. Chweh, *Book Editor*

David L. Bender, *Publisher*
Bruno Leone, *Executive Editor*
Bonnie Szumski, *Series Editor*

Greenhaven Press, Inc., San Diego, CA

Every effort has been made to trace the owners of copyrighted material. The articles in this volume may have been edited for content, length, and/or reading level. The titles have been changed to enhance the editorial purpose. Those interested in locating the original source will find the complete citation on the first page of each article.

Library of Congress Cataloging-in-Publication Data

Readings on Cyrano de Bergerac / Crystal R. Chweh,
    book editor.
        p. cm. — (The Greenhaven Press literary
companion to world literature)
        title: Cyrano de Bergerac.
        Includes bibliographical references and index.
        ISBN 0-7377-0433-0 (pbk. : alk. paper) —
ISBN 0-7377-0434-9 (lib. bdg. : alk. paper)
        1. Rostand, Edmond, 1868–1918. Cyrano de Bergerac.
2. Cyrano de Bergerac, 1619–1655—In literature. I. Title:
Cyrano de Bergerac. II. Chweh, Crystal R. III. Series

PQ2635.O7 C947 2001
842'.8—dc21

                                                    00-041074

Cover photo: © Roger-Viollet/Gamma/Liaison Agency

Copyright © 2001 by Greenhaven Press, Inc.
PO Box 289009
San Diego, CA 92198-9009
Printed in the U.S.A.

" To joke in the face of danger is the supreme politeness, a delicate refusal to cast oneself as a tragic hero; panache is therefore a timid heroism, like the smile with which one excuses one's superiority. "

—Edmond Rostand

CONTENTS

Chapter 1: Creating a Comedy-Heroic

Chapter 2: Major Themes

FOREWORD

*"'Tis the good reader that
makes the good book."*

Ralph Waldo Emerson

The story's bare facts are simple: The captain, an old and scarred seafarer, walks with a peg leg made of whale ivory. He relentlessly drives his crew to hunt the world's oceans for the great white whale that crippled him. After a long search, the ship encounters the whale and a fierce battle ensues. Finally the captain drives his harpoon into the whale, but the harpoon line catches the captain about the neck and drags him to his death.

A simple story, a straightforward plot—yet, since the 1851 publication of Herman Melville's *Moby-Dick*, readers and critics have found many meanings in the struggle between Captain Ahab and the whale. To some, the novel is a cautionary tale that depicts how Ahab's obsession with revenge leads to his insanity and death. Others believe that the whale represents the unknowable secrets of the universe and that Ahab is a tragic hero who dares to challenge fate by attempting to discover this knowledge. Perhaps Melville intended Ahab as a criticism of Americans' tendency to become involved in well-intentioned but irrational causes. Or did Melville model Ahab after himself, letting his fictional character express his anger at what he perceived as a cruel and distant god?

Although literary critics disagree over the meaning of *Moby-Dick*, readers do not need to choose one particular interpretation in order to gain an understanding of Melville's novel. Instead, by examining various analyses, they can gain numerous insights into the issues that lie under the surface of the basic plot. Studying the writings of literary critics can also aid readers in making their own assessments of *Moby-Dick* and other literary works and in developing analytical thinking skills.

The Greenhaven Literary Companion Series was created with these goals in mind. Designed for young adults, this unique anthology series provides an engaging and comprehensive introduction to literary analysis and criticism. The essays included in the Literary Companion Series are chosen for their accessibility to a young adult audience and are expertly edited in consideration of both the reading and comprehension levels of this audience. In addition, each essay is introduced by a concise summation that presents the contributing writer's main themes and insights. Every anthology in the Literary Companion Series contains a varied selection of critical essays that cover a wide time span and express diverse views. Wherever possible, primary sources are represented through excerpts from authors' notebooks, letters, and journals and through contemporary criticism.

Each title in the Literary Companion Series pays careful consideration to the historical context of the particular author or literary work. In-depth biographies and detailed chronologies reveal important aspects of authors' lives and emphasize the historical events and social milieu that influenced their writings. To facilitate further research, every anthology includes primary and secondary source bibliographies of articles and/or books selected for their suitability for young adults. These engaging features make the Greenhaven Literary Companion series ideal for introducing students to literary analysis in the classroom or as a library resource for young adults researching the world's great authors and literature.

Exceptional in its focus on young adults, the Greenhaven Literary Companion Series strives to present literary criticism in a compelling and accessible format. Every title in the series is intended to spark readers' interest in leading American and world authors, to help them broaden their understanding of literature, and to encourage them to formulate their own analyses of the literary works that they read. It is the editors' hope that young adult readers will find these anthologies to be true companions in their study of literature.

INTRODUCTION

When put to the test, Edmond Rostand's play *Cyrano de Bergerac* offers up an apparent tangle of conflicting perspectives to the modern reader. The play takes the conventional fairy tale of "handsome prince plus beautiful maiden equals happily ever after" and gives it a twist. Hence, in spite of his accomplishments, Cyrano, the larger-than-life hero—swordsman, philosopher, and poet—is not as handsome as he would like to be. Roxane, the beautiful, witty, and resourceful heroine, follows suit and falls in love with a handsome man (Christian) who cannot meet her intellectual needs. Further upsetting expectations, Rostand solidifies this as a truly bizarre love triangle when Cyrano volunteers to help Christian woo Roxane. After these developments, the unqualified happily-ever-after ending seems rather unlikely for our hero, and in fact, Rostand ultimately denies all three characters that elusive prize.

So how does *Cyrano de Bergerac* persist in selling itself as a romantic, popular play? Certainly, persistence, along with a healthy dose of comedy and nonstop action, is the key. To the reader, Cyrano persists in being Roxane's true soul mate even as he spends most of his time aiding Christian's efforts. With unbelievable cleverness and eloquence, Cyrano can compose a rhymed, metered poem while fighting a duel. He can fight a hundred men single-handedly and emerge victorious. He overwhelmingly proves himself to be worthy of Roxane's admiration. And, while Cyrano cannot claim to have the most pure motives—frustration, envy, and jealousy might weigh in equally with love, honor, and friendship—he can claim to be extraordinary *and* human. In this way, Rostand succeeds in convincing his readers that his paragon hero with the nose complex is in reality the ever popular and misunderstood underdog.

On a grander scale, *Cyrano de Bergerac* has established itself as a cultural phenomenon. Cyrano, with his panache, is what some call the epitome of a French hero. People aspire to be like Cyrano, and he is a cultural byword in France for leadership. But English-speaking nations can probably claim a second ownership. The United States can be relied on to produce a *Cyrano*-based plot on the silver screen every couple of years and a stage production much more frequently than that. *Cyrano de Bergerac* is also at the heart of various musical endeavors, ranging from rock to opera.

Rostand's critics, however, have not let the play's ubiquity alone decide its literary merit. They point out the impossible situations that Rostand expects readers to believe: for example, Roxane's unexpected appearance at the siege or Cyrano's aforementioned poetic duel. Critics who have dissected *Cyrano de Bergerac* point out that it is made up of disjointed pieces with numerous individual weaknesses. Others point out the moral quicksand that Cyrano stands in when deceiving Roxane for Christian, whom she even marries. But very few critics, faced with the far-reaching impact of Rostand's play, can entirely dismiss the play's effect on its audience, emotionally and psychologically. Cyrano's panache, coupled with his self-doubt, makes him an ideal theatrical character— one that runs the gamut of emotional extremes. Furthermore, some critics suggest that, in some ways, the play's superior theatricality lets it accomplish feats that other plays of greater literary standing cannot.

The essays in this volume investigate such critics' often polar viewpoints and explore the different facets of the play that have made it an enduring work of literature. They take on the task of sorting out the puzzle that is *Cyrano de Bergerac* and also try to examine why some people like the play while others do not—a deceptively simple question. The play's unraveling in this manner will hopefully enlighten as well as intrigue the reader.

EDMOND ROSTAND: A BIOGRAPHY

When writing *Cyrano de Bergerac*, Edmond Rostand took a chance and broke away from the stylistic trends of his time. While others in the late nineteenth century were describing, in great detail, the harsh realities of life, Rostand wrote stories with fairy-tale plots and fantastical characters. He tried to create works that he could admire and with which he could feel proud to associate. Rostand wrote only a handful of plays and poems, and, of those, only *Cyrano de Bergerac* was an unqualified success. It was enough, however, to justify his reception into the French Academy at the age of only thirty-three. Even as the decades pass, Rostand's creative gift of Cyrano to French culture and cultures worldwide remains incalculable.

EARLY LIFE

Edmond Rostand was born on April 1, 1868, in Marseille, a major French port on the Mediterranean Sea and the oldest city in France. The harbor of Marseille, from the time of the Crusaders, has welcomed far-flung vessels—from such places as Italy, Asia, and Africa. This seaport did not lack for exotic and varied influences with which to fuel Rostand's imagination.

Rostand came from a distinguished family. Known for their interest and support of artistic and literary pursuits, they mainly made their living as merchants and bankers. Speculation has it that Beethoven's quartets were first played in France in the home of a Rostand. Poetry ran in the family. Rostand's aunt, Victorine, had a volume of verses published in 1844. Edmond's father, Eugène Rostand, a prominent journalist and economist, was also literary. He published essays on economic subjects, translated the Roman poet Catullus into French verse, and produced several volumes of original poetry.

Early schooling for Rostand took place in Marseille. There, encouraged by an assistant teacher, he began to write his own poetry. He studied classical and contemporary poets. He received many prizes in French and in history and founded a school newspaper, which lasted for five issues.

A TALENTED STUDENT

In 1884 Rostand moved to Paris to complete his secondary school education at the Collège Stanislas, where he took classes in French literature, history, and philosophy. In Paris, Rostand had the opportunity to study with René Doumic, a famous French literary critic of the 1880s and 1890s. Doumic spoke of him with high praise, reporting that although Rostand was given to fantasy, he nevertheless surpassed all of his classmates in composition. It is likely that in his studies with Doumic, Rostand first learned of the real Cyrano. While in Paris, he also attended the literary salon of the celebrated poet Leconte de Lisle.

In 1887 Rostand's scholastic aptitude won him the Marshal de Villar Prize, given by the Academy of Marseille, for his essay "Two Novelists of Provence: Honoré d'Urfé and Émile Zola." Rostand mentions d'Urfé, a seventeenth-century writer of pastoral romances, several times in *Cyrano de Bergerac.*

After earning his bachelor's degree, Rostand began his law studies. He also worked briefly in a bank, but poetry was his foremost love. Fortunately for Rostand, his prosperous and supportive family made it so that he did not have to work for a living. This might partially account for the scarcity of his works and why, although he gained admission to the bar in Paris, he never practiced law. He could afford to pursue his literary interests at his leisure.

THE LITERARY ATMOSPHERE

France, perhaps reflecting the sentiment stirred up by the disastrous Franco-Prussian War of 1870, had developed a trend in which its writers sought to discover in the contemporary political, social, and industrial situation the causes of the nation's spiritual misery. Along these lines, Émile Zola developed a series of experimental novels that proposed to lay bare "the sores" of contemporary French society.

With more art than patriotism in mind, André Antoine founded the Théâtre Libre (Free Theater) in 1887. The theater operated by selling season subscriptions to spectators. In this manner, the authors and actors sidestepped intervention from public censorship. Proposing to present a "slice of life,"

Antoine insisted on the removal of all traditional dramatic convention. For example, the actor aimed at acting as though he or she was unaware of the audience. This precursor to method acting also prescribed being the part, not just acting it. Eventually, however, this trend in modern theater, in its extreme, with its focus on bare-bones realities, began to tire audiences.

ROMANCE THRIVES

Rostand deliberately chose to dissociate his writing from his contemporaries' somber pessimism and championed a return to romantic themes. Romance flourished in Rostand's personal life as well. In 1888, at Luchon in the Pyrenees, where Rostand often spent his summer vacations, he met Rosemonde Gérard, a poet and the granddaughter of Marshal Gérard. That same year, Rostand collaborated with Rosemonde's half brother and created *Le Gant Rouge* (The Red Glove), a prose comedy in four acts. The play debuted at Cluny Theater. It showed fifteen times during the summer of 1889 and received little acclaim.

Rostand married Rosemonde and settled in Paris in 1890. His wedding gift to her was his first volume of poetry, *Les Musardises* (The Idlers), published that year at the couple's expense. While well received by a small public and favorably reviewed by the critics, it had little impact and sold very few copies. Rosemonde's verses received much acclaim of their own. Throughout their life together, Rosemonde, a discriminating critic of great originality, provided a great deal of help to her husband.

LAUNCHING A LITERARY CAREER

Rosemonde was also an actress. She performed in Rostand's first poetic play, *Les Deux Pierrots* (The Two Pierrots). In this fantasy, one Pierrot (a stock comic character of old French pantomimes) laughs and one cries. Rostand presented his one-act farce to the Comédie Française (the state-subsidized national theater of France and one of France's most influential and cherished cultural institutions) in 1891. Initially, the theater accepted the play, but when members of the theater's reading committee pointed out its stylistic similarities to the work of another dramatist who had just died, Rostand withdrew the play. Soon after this, noted theater critic Jules Claretie said to Rostand, "Bring me another act." (*Act* in French may also mean "one-act play.") The young poet responded, "I shall bring you two."[1] A few weeks later he had written *Les Romanesques* (The Romantics), which was performed two years later.

With *Les Romanesques*, a three-act comedy in verse, Rostand received the distinction of having a play show at the Comédie Française. This play, after a minor revision, was unanimously accepted. It debuted in 1894, brought him to public attention, and won a prize of five thousand francs. The story is a fantasy satire of William Shakespeare's *Romeo and Juliet*. In this version, parents pretend to be enemies to ensure that their children fall in love. Ultimately, the characters come to the conclusion that true romance must be found within, despite whatever real or apparent danger exists. (An offshoot of this play in the United States is the long-running 1960s musical adaptation The Fantasticks.)

The next year *La Princess Lointaine* (The Faraway Princess), a four-act play in verse, debuted on April 5. It was acted by the famed French actress Sarah Bernhardt, for whom Rostand wrote the play, in her own theater, the Renaissance. The hero of this play is the same troubadour, Joffrey Rudel, whom Romantic poet Robert Browning chose to write about in his *Rudel to the Lady of Tripoli*. The play marks Rostand's turn from humorous satire and fantasy to more serious and romantic themes. It relates the ancient tale of Joffrey's love for Mélissande, the princess of Tripoli. This play was considered a critical success, although its idealism is heavily laden with sentimentality. Still, Rostand's name and influence spread. His success brought with it the honor of having Benoît-Constant Coquelin, the greatest French comic actor of the period, to ask Rostand to write him a play—an effort that would eventually become *Cyrano de Bergerac*.

FAILING HEALTH AND CONTROVERSY

Pressure and fame took their toll, however. In 1896 Rostand suffered from neurasthenia, an emotional and psychological disorder, which signaled the beginning of his bouts with ill health that would trouble him for the rest of his life. Also at this time, the Dreyfus Affair, the controversy involving the French army officer Alfred Dreyfus, who was convicted on a charge of treason, shook France. Rostand, although not at the forefront of the cause, labeled himself a Dreyfusard, meaning that he felt Dreyfus had been the victim of a miscarriage of justice. Fortunately for him, the negative backlash that such a stand had on other Dreyfusards did not seem to touch his popularity.

On April 14, 1897, Rostand's biblical piece in three tableaus, *La Samaritaine* (The Woman of Samaria), debuted. This play, also written for Sarah Bernhardt, opened at the Renaissance Theater. The story, drawn from the fourth chapter of the book of John, centers around the Samarian woman at the well and Jesus Christ, who converts her. *La Samaritaine* had some success, largely due to Bernhardt's interpretation. The success of both the characters of Mélissande and the woman of Samaria owed much to Bernhardt's participation. However, some critics at the time felt that the play overly humanized Christ, in part by making him too much the Romantic poet.

Cyrano de Bergerac, A Labor of Love

Many factors went into the creation of *Cyrano de Bergerac*. Rostand had learned about the historical character of Savinien de Cyrano de Bergerac through his earlier classical studies. Another contemporary influence was a farce, *Roquelaure, ou L'homme le Plus Laid de France* (Roquelaure, or the Ugliest Man in France), which appeared in 1836.

Rostand's wife, Rosemonde, offered an anecdote for further motivation for *Cyrano de Bergerac*. One summer in Luchon, in the Pyrenees, Rostand met a young man who was suffering from unrequited love. The lovesick young man told Rostand that he had done his best, but the woman he loved was indifferent to him. Rostand asked him what he said to the young woman. The man replied,

> "I tell her that I love her."
> "And then?"
> "I begin all over again."
> "And after that?"
> "That's all there is."[2]

Rostand offered his help. He began coaching the young man in speech, literary allusions, and style. The coaching worked and the young man won his suit.

Attention to Detail

When creating *Cyrano de Bergerac*, Rostand captured the spirit of the seventeenth century rather than its grim reality. Real places and people functioned only as springboards, which he did not mean to be accurate portrayals of historical figures. However, he found the basis for characters such as Cyrano, Le Bret, Christian, and Roxane in the real-life personages of Savinien de Cyrano de Bergerac; Henri Le Bret; Christophe de Champagne, baron de Neuvillette; and Madeleine Robineau.

The real Savinien de Cyrano de Bergerac provided Rostand with the inspiration of having the romantic contrast of a noble soul in a less-than-perfect body. Cyrano de Bergerac was born near Paris in 1619 and was reputed to have a rather large nose. He met his friend Henri Le Bret while attending private school in the country. He enlisted with the guardsmen of Captain Carbon de Castel-Jaloux in 1638. Wounded at the siege of Arras—as mirrored in *Cyrano de Bergerac*—he was known for his temper and belligerence. Rostand took these seeming contradictions and demonstrated their effectiveness in creating a popular hero.

AN IMMEDIATE SUCCESS

In general, *Cyrano*'s quick and complex action, its lyrical and dramatic brilliancy, and its stylish sentiment and wit continue to charm audiences even after works of greater literary merit slowly fall out of common circulation. *Cyrano* was important to the drama of its time because of its romantic nature, which departed from the realistic conventions then in vogue. Rostand's mingling of historical accuracies and inaccuracies, however, offered the kind of creation that would also satisfy minds accustomed to realistic and naturalistic drama. In *Cyrano*, Rostand's writing is said to blend "the grotesque and the sublime, the dramatic and the lyric, the ugly and the beautiful."[3]

Another part of *Cyrano*'s charm is its suitability for the stage. The seventeenth-century setting is full of luxurious color and movement. Cyrano fits right in as a larger-than-life character—the great swashbuckling hero. As T.S. Eliot said regarding the playwright, "With Rostand, the center of gravity is in the expression of emotion."[4] Emotions play a large role in the play without overburdening the audience with suffocating sentiment. Rostand works artfully with the irony of Cyrano's tragic story, making light of his character's troubles, even in the most pitiable situations. This balance provides the counterpoint that keeps even modern readers and audiences intrigued.

Cyrano's immense popularity has led to its translation from French into many languages: German, Swedish, Spanish, Portuguese, English, Polish, Russian, Catalan, Japanese, Afrikaans, Italian, Arabic, Hebrew, and Korean—to name a few. It continues to be adapted for film, television, as a musical (lyrics adapted by British author Anthony Burgess), and as an opera (by Walter Damrosch). Many famous actors have performed the role of Cyrano, including Coquelin, Gérard Depardieu, Richard Mansfield, Walter Hampden, and José Ferrer.

CRITICAL ACCLAIM

1897 marked a busy year for Rostand. On December 27 *Cyrano de Bergerac* opened, with Coquelin playing Cyrano. And once again, Rosemonde helped her husband out of a difficult situation by acting. Rostand needed her to play Roxane on *Cyrano*'s opening night, when the scheduled actress fell ill. Without further rehearsal—she fortunately knew the part by heart—she was able to perform the role.

The final dress rehearsal of *Cyrano de Bergerac* took place at the Porte-Saint-Martin Theater on its opening night, December 27, 1897. Fifteen minutes before curtain, suffering from nerves, Rostand said to Coquelin, "I beg your forgiveness. Pardon me, my friend, for having involved you in this disastrous adventure!"[5] But at two o'clock in the morning following the first night's performance, the audience, still in a wild state of excitement, cried, applauded, and refused to leave the theater. The play was an instant success, so much so that its audiences often began learning the lines by heart. One night, a tired Coquelin omitted four lines, only to have a member of the audience catch the omission and demand the full text. Coquelin smiled and bowed, saying, "You are right, sir. I shall go back and repeat."[6] When he finished, the performance was interrupted for several minutes by waves of applause.

Rostand was only twenty-nine years old when *Cyrano* debuted, and at this young age he was catapulted into fame. *Cyrano*'s production marks the peak of his career. The play opened with an amazing five hundred consecutive performances. And enthusiastic critics hailed Rostand as the legitimate successor to Victor Hugo, Molière, and Shakespeare. Very soon after *Cyrano*'s opening night, Félix-Jules Méline, France's premier, decorated Rostand as a knight of the Legion of Honor—a French order of merit awarded for outstanding achievements in military or civil life. As a testament to the strength of Rostand's unfailing idealism, *Cyrano* is still one of the most popular and well-known French plays of all time.

AFTER *CYRANO*

For his next project, Rostand took on the task of creating a fully tragic hero. Produced in 1900, *L'Aiglon* (*The Eaglet*) tells the tale of Napoléon's son, imprisoned in Austria until his death in 1832. Sarah Bernhardt first played the lead role in France; Maude Adams created the role of the tragic child in the United States. In this play, Rostand's swashbuckling vivacity and fanciful humor are somewhat tamed, and the characterization might be said to be more complete, although its hero is less impressive. Some critics believe that *L'Aiglon* shows Rostand's growing sophistication by consciously following a more unified story. At the time, the play met with modest success in France but much less enthusiasm elsewhere.

As the new century progressed, Rostand's neurasthenia worsened and became compounded with mild bronchial pneumonia. His doctor advised him to move to a milder climate. In 1900 he went with his wife and his two sons to Basque country on the border of France and Spain. First staying at a health retreat, they later moved to a large house, named Arnaga, that Rostand had built in the Basque style near the village of Cambo-les-Bains on the lower slopes of the Pyrenees.

On May 30, 1901, Rostand received the honor of election to the French Academy at the age of thirty-three, the youngest member at that time; the academy bestowed on him a "Grand Diploma." Illness, however, postponed his official reception ceremony until June 4, 1903, when Vicomte Eugenè-Melchior de Vogüé officiated. In 1901 Rostand was also made an officer of the Legion of Honor (he was made a commander of the Legion of Honor in 1910).

ROSTAND THE PERFECTIONIST

In the following years, Rostand's productivity slowed markedly. He continued to live at Cambo-les-Bains, and there he wrote *Chantecler* in 1908. The allegorical play, which takes place in a barnyard, took Rostand ten years to write—partly because of failing health.

As a writer, Rostand did not like to be distracted from his work. Rosemonde related how Rostand would frequently withdraw from a social evening, saying, "I have to go home. I am tired."[7] He would return home quickly and then, instead of retiring, would take up paper and pen, finding relief in his work.

Rostand tired easily, but he took painstaking care with his writing. He spent years polishing individual lines of verse and perfecting his style. As one critic put it, "He [Rostand] lives for his art alone, and deigns to allow his plays to become public property only after they have undergone the most minute and painstaking revision."[8] Like *Cyrano de Bergerac*, Rostand wrote *Chantecler* for Coquelin. However, tormented by qualms, Rostand did not give *Chantecler* to Coquelin until the end of 1908. Coquelin's death in 1909, shortly before the play's first scheduled performance, further slowed the play's production. With Coquelin's death, Rostand lost a great friend and a precious resource of knowledge about the theater. Maude Adams, a popular American actor, eventually created the lead for the United States.

In spite of the lengthy time it took Rostand to produce *Chantecler*, he retained his reputation as a master of poetic drama in France, and his admirers continued to eagerly look forward to his next work. During the years preceding the production of *Chantecler*, newspaper stories often appeared relating how the play was held back until four lines in the third act met with Rostand's approval.

Whatever his shortcomings, Rostand set high goals for himself and his work. He described *Chantecler* as "the drama of human endeavor grappling with life"[9]—no small experience to dramatize. *Chantecler*'s hero is the rooster of the barnyard, who believes his crowing causes the sun to rise. Other characters include the birds and animals of the farmyard and forest. For their models, Rostand used his knowledge of the literary circles of Paris. The play tries to present the idea of the beauty of life lived for an ideal. But Parisian audiences, after satisfying their curiosity, soon lost interest in it and its message. According to one critic, after all the publicity leading up to the play, "even a *Macbeth* or an *Oedipus* would have disappointed the public."[10]

In 1910 Rostand produced a parody on the gods of ancient Greece, *Le Bois Sacré* (The Sacred Wood). It was a pantomime, accompanied by a poem and produced at the Sarah Bernhardt Theater. In 1911 he began work on *La Dernière Nuit de Don Juan* (The Last Night of Don Juan). This play, an unflattering look at Don Juan's amatory career, would not be performed in his lifetime.

The poor reception of the later works still did not seem to dent Rostand's reputation. Audiences continued to revere him as the creator of *Cyrano* and the accolades followed. In

1913 *Cyrano* received the honor of a Paris revival—with much fanfare and affection—for its thousandth performance.

FINAL DAYS

When World War I broke out, Rostand was refused entrance in the French army because of his poor health. However, he intensely followed the war and even visited the front in 1915. He also wrote *Le Vol de la Marseillaise,* a large volume of patriotic poetry, at this time.

In these latter years, Rostand's poor health often kept him in bed until late each morning reading. Sometimes, after meals, he would spend time with his family, reading passages from books and plays out loud. In the late afternoon, he would often stroll through his garden to admire a trio of statues—busts of Shakespeare, Victor Hugo, and Cervantes, great writers who had been his models.

On December 2, 1918, shortly after the end of World War I, Edmond Rostand died, succumbing at last to his battle with respiratory ailments. He was survived by Rosemonde and his two sons, both of whom would lead distinguished careers: Jean as a scientist and Maurice as a literary critic and novelist.

NOTES

1. Quoted in Barrett H. Clark, *Contemporary French Dramatists.* Cincinnati, OH: Stewart and Kidd, 1916, p. 104.
2. Quoted in Helen Louise Cohen, *Milestones of the Drama.* New York: Harcourt, Brace & World, 1940, p. 352.
3. Colbert Searles, ed., *Seven French Plays.* New York: Henry Holt, 1935, p. 592.
4. Quoted in John Gassner, ed., *A Treasure of the Theatre.* New York: Simon and Schuster, 1967, p. 275.
5. Edmond Rostand, *Cyrano de Bergerac,* ed. Geoff Woollen. London: Bristol Classical, 1994, p. ix.
6. Quoted in Cohen, *Milestones of the Drama,* p. 351.
7. Quoted in Cohen, *Milestones of the Drama,* p. 352.
8. Quoted in Clark, *Contemporary French Dramatists,* p. 120.
9. Quoted in Clark, *Contemporary French Dramatists,* p. 118.
10. Quoted in Albert Bermel, ed., *The Genius of the French Theater.* New York: New American Library, 1961, p. 373.

Characters and Plot

The Characters

Bellerose. The manager of the theater where Montfleury acts.

Cyrano de Bergerac. The play's main character, who is in love with his cousin Roxane. Cyrano is known for his unusually large nose and quick temper. He is a talented musician, poet, swordsman, and philosopher. His unwillingness to compromise or sully his ideals motivates his character. His panache, sometimes represented as his white plume, symbolizes nobility and grace even in the face of death—idealistic, heroic values.

Carbon de Castel-Jaloux. Captain of the Gascon Cadets, to which Cyrano belongs. He regards Cyrano as a trusted adviser.

Cuigy and Brissaille. Friends of Cyrano.

Comte de Guiche. A powerful nobleman who is infatuated with Roxane. He comes into conflict with Cyrano over this issue and because of their differing politics. He frequently uses his extensive influence to exact revenge or get his own way.

Mère Marguerite de Jésus. Mother Superior of the Park of the Sisters of the Holy Cross.

Jodelet. An actor at the theater where Montfleury acts.

Le Bret. Cyrano's loyal friend and confidant. He is the only one who points out Cyrano's shortcomings and who tries to look after his best interests.

Lignière. A poet and a friend of Cyrano. He writes a scathing poem about de Guiche, who retaliates by sending one hundred men to ambush the poet. Cyrano fights all the men at once to save Lignière's life.

Lise. Ragueneau's wife. When she runs off with a musketeer, Ragueneau leaves his bakery and takes a job in Roxane's household.

Montfleury. An actor at the Hall of the Hôtel de Bourgogne. Cyrano prohibits him from performing for three weeks as punishment for inappropriately admiring Roxane.

Christian de Neuvillette. A cadet in Cyrano's company. He loves Roxane but lacks the ability to impress her intellectually. He is brave and has a noble spirit, but he struggles with his limitations. He obtains Cyrano's help to win Roxane's love, but the deception places him in the strange position of being the rival of his supposed self, which is really a combination of his good looks and Cyrano's intelligence. His integrity makes it difficult to accept that deception.

Ragueneau. A friend to Cyrano and Roxane. Initially, the poetic owner of a pastry shop. Later, he holds many jobs, including singer, bathhouse attendant, and hairdresser.

Roxane (also Magdeleine Robin). The *précieuse* (intellectual) and beauty who inspires different kinds of love in Cyrano, Christian, and de Guiche. She falls in love with Christian's beauty and, unknowingly, Cyrano's soul. She is a romantic with demanding standards, and she highly values a well-turned phrase. She often turns a situation to her own advantage through clever planning.

Sister Marthe and Sister Claire. Nuns in the Park of the Sisters of the Holy Cross, where Roxane takes up residence late in the play.

Vicomte de Valvert. A pawn and toady for de Guiche. He is originally intended to be Roxane's husband.

The Plot

Some translations might not break the play into scenes, only acts. This should not affect the use of this summary, which sequentially follows the play's action.

Act 1—A Performance at the Hôtel de Bourgogne. Scene 1. In the Hall of the Hôtel de Bourgogne in 1640, an audience assembles in anticipation of the performance of a play, *La Clorise.* Among them, groups of people engage in various activities: cavaliers try to enter for free, servants gamble and flirt, a thief picks pockets, a citizen and his son discuss the play, and some noblemen enter.

Scene 2. Lignière, a baker, introduces Christian de Neuvillette to the noblemen. Christian announces that he is newly arrived to Paris and will join the ranks of the Cadets tomorrow. He talks with the noblemen, who are people-watching. Christian reveals that he is looking for a lady (Roxane), whom he has admired even though he does not know her name. While waiting for Roxane to arrive, Lignière introduces Christian to Ragueneau, a baker and poet. Ragueneau reveals that his friend Cyrano de Bergerac, the famed poet and swordsman, has forbidden Montfleury, the actor starring in the play, to appear on stage for the next three weeks because of his hatred for him. Montfleury intends to perform tonight, so they speculate over whether Cyrano will make an appearance.

Le Bret is introduced and joins others in praising Cyrano as an extraordinary and talented man. Ragueneau warns, however, that Cyrano has an extraordinarily large nose and tends to fight (with great skill) those who ridicule or comment on it.

Christian spots Roxane, and Lignière identifies her as an unmarried orphan and Cyrano's cousin. Christian—handsome but not eloquent—is dismayed when Lignière describes Roxane as an intellectual (*précieuse*). Lignière points out that Roxane is now observing Christian and tells Christian that the married Comte de Guiche is in love with Roxane. De Guiche wants Roxane to marry a man under his influence, Monsieur de Valvert, who will not object to de Guiche having a discreet affair with her after their marriage. Lignière brags that he has written an unflattering poem about de Guiche.

Scene 3. Lignière points out to Christian the powerful de Guiche and his court of sycophants (Valvert among them). As Christian contemplates challenging Valvert to a duel, he discovers that he is being pickpocketed. He catches the thief, who tries to barter for his freedom by revealing that Lignière is in danger for writing his inflammatory poem. A hundred men have been hired to ambush him on his way home. Christian is diverted from his duel and leaves to find and warn Lignière. The audience gets rowdy and wants the play to start. Montfleury appears and begins to speak. A voice interrupts and demands that he leave the stage. Montfleury refuses. The concealed speaker stands and reveals himself to be Cyrano.

Scene 4. Montfleury asks the noblemen for protection and remains on stage. Cyrano continues to urge the actor to leave and issues a challenge to the entire audience: Anyone who objects can fight Cyrano in a duel. His reputation as a swordsman is well known, and no one takes up his offer. Montfleury leaves the stage. The citizen's son (who had been discussing the upcoming play earlier with his father) asks Cyrano why he has done this. Cyrano replies that the first reason is that Montfleury is a bad actor and that the second reason is a secret. Cyrano gives Bellerose, the theater manager, money to compensate him for the night's lost revenue.

A busybody tells Cyrano that Montfleury has a powerful patron. Cyrano replies that he also has a powerful patron: his sword. De Guiche, who has been observing the argument, tires of Cyrano's actions and prompts Valvert to intervene. Valvert unimaginatively insults Cyrano's nose. Cyrano is unimpressed and launches into an impressive monologue describing the myriad ways his nose could have been more properly insulted. Valvert responds by insulting Cyrano's plain clothing. Attire was, at that time, indicative of class and distinction—the more elaborate, the more important the person. Cyrano asserts that his inner distinctions are more important and initiates a duel with Valvert.

In this highlight of the play, Cyrano, while fighting, composes a poem that he impressively manages to coordinate with the fight. At the end of each refrain, as promised, he gets past Valvert's defenses with his sword, a touch or a hit. Cyrano wins the duel. D'Artagnan, the famous musketeer from Alexandre Dumas's novel *The Three Musketeers*, congratulates Cyrano.

Cyrano reveals to Le Bret that he has no money for food. He gave all his next month's income away when he paid Bellerose, as a fine gesture. A girl selling food offers him whatever he wishes for free. Cyrano takes only a single grape, a glass of water, and half a macaroon. He gallantly kisses the girl's hand for her generosity.

Scene 5. As Cyrano eats, Le Bret warns him that he is making powerful enemies. Cyrano dismisses this and reveals that his actions that night were prompted by Montfleury's attentions to Roxane, his cousin and the woman he secretly loves. Cyrano believes himself too ugly to win Roxane's affection. Le Bret urges Cyrano to confess his love to Roxane and cites the admiring girl who gave him his food earlier as proof that love can come to anyone.

Scene 6. Almost as if to support Le Bret's theory, Roxane's chaperon suddenly appears and tells him that Roxane wishes to meet Cyrano privately. Cyrano is completely astonished and tells her that Roxane should meet him at Ragueneau's bakery tomorrow. He agrees to be there at seven o'clock in the morning.

Scene 7. Cyrano is ecstatic. He leaves the theater with Le

Bret and meets Lignière, who knows about the hundred men waiting to ambush him and is afraid to go home. Cyrano volunteers to escort Lignière home. They gain a crowd of spectators as they go, but Cyrano warns them that he wants to take on the hundred men alone. He boasts that so many men were necessary because it is known that Lignière is *his* friend.

Act 2—The Poets' Bakery. Scene 1. At Ragueneau's shop, pastry chefs are busy working. Ragueneau writes poetry amidst the activity. Lise, Ragueneau's wife, more pragmatic, has made paper bags out of poems, which were left by Ragueneau's friends as payment for pastries.

Scene 2. Two children enter and buy pastries. Ragueneau follows them out and gives them extra pastries in exchange for the pastries' wrapper. Cyrano enters the shop.

Scene 3. Ragueneau praises Cyrano for his poetic duel, quoting from it. Cyrano is anxious about Roxane's arrival. He decides to write her a letter that expresses his feelings for her.

Scene 4. While Cyrano writes his declaration of love, Ragueneau's poet friends arrive—hungry. They bring reports of the aftermath of the battle with the hundred men. They heard that one man had accomplished the feat, but they do not realize that it was Cyrano. They passed through the battle site on their way over and saw proof of Cyrano's victory— abandoned weapons, clothing, and even dead bodies. Ragueneau recites a poem, which is a rhyming recipe. Cyrano observes that the hungry poets are sneaking food and warns Ragueneau. Ragueneau generously replies that he is just as pleased when they like his food as when they admire his poems. All the while, Lise and a musketeer in the shop have been flirting. Cyrano warns the man away. At Cyrano's signal, Ragueneau clears the shop for Roxane's arrival.

Scene 5. Cyrano decides that he will produce his letter if Roxane shows any sign of encouragement. Roxane arrives in disguise, and Cyrano bribes her chaperon to leave them alone by giving the duenna pastries.

Scene 6. Alone with Roxane, Cyrano asks her why she has asked to meet him privately. Roxane begins by praising his duel at the theater and then, uncomfortable, tries to set herself at ease by recalling the time they spent together as children. She likens him to a brother, one who did whatever she asked. She remembers that she used to play mother and scold him when he injured himself.

She takes his hand and sees a wound from his battle the night before with the hundred men. She begins to doctor it and asks him to tell her what happened. He, in turn, demands that she tell him why she is meeting with him. She finishes bandaging his hand and confesses that she loves someone who is proud, noble, brave, and beautiful.

Cyrano realizes that his hopes have been in vain. Although she has only admired him from afar, Roxane claims to love Baron Christian de Neuvillette, a new member of Cyrano's regiment. Cyrano asks her if she has considered that Christian might not be an intellectual like herself. She refuses to believe that someone who looks as heroic as Christian could possibly be less than perfect.

Cyrano says that he does not see why her revelation required this meeting. Roxane replies that she has heard that his regiment is made of Gascons and that they pick fights with newcomers who are not pure-blooded Gascons. She asks him to protect Christian and keep him safe from duels. Cyrano promises. On her way out, Roxane half-heartedly praises Cyrano's defeat of the hundred men, but her real concern is to have Cyrano instruct Christian to write her a letter.

Scene 7. Ragueneau returns and the captain of the Cadets, Carbon de Castel-Jaloux, arrives praising Cyrano's now infamous hundred-man battle. The rest of his company, the Cadets, arrives. Christian is among them. An admiring crowd comes looking for Cyrano. Cyrano is still upset over his rendezvous and is uninterested. De Guiche arrives and offers the prestige of his patronage and perhaps that of his powerful uncle, the Cardinal Richelieu. Cyrano has a play he wants produced and is tempted, but de Guiche mentions that to accomplish that, his uncle would want to rewrite a few lines. Cyrano refuses his offer. De Guiche reveals that he was behind the plot to ambush Lignière. As de Guiche leaves, he compares Cyrano to Don Quixote, suggesting that picking fights with enemies is like tilting at windmills: One may joust the blades of the windmill, but they will come full circle and cast the hero down into the mire.

Scene 8. Le Bret reproaches Cyrano for alienating a powerful patron. Cyrano launches into a stirring speech about being independent, being alone. Le Bret correctly guesses that behind this speech is bitterness and pride over unrequited love.

Scene 9. Because Christian is not a Gascon, the Cadets ignore him except to insult him and warn him not to mention

Cyrano's nose. As Cyrano finally begins telling his tale of the night before to a crowd of Cadets, Christian, to prove his courage in front of the Cadets, deliberately interrupts by interjecting "nose" throughout Cyrano's recitation. Cyrano, remembering his promise to Roxane, tries to conceal his anger, but eventually he clears the room, leaving himself alone with Christian.

Scene 10. Cyrano reveals that he is Roxane's cousin, and Christian apologizes for his insults. Cyrano tells him of Roxane's desire for a letter. Christian replies that he can be clever enough with insults, but he is tongue-tied when it comes to wooing. Cyrano reflects that he is clever enough but lacks Christian's looks. Cyrano devises a plan: combining their attributes, they will woo Roxane together. Cyrano will compose the words for Christian, starting with the letter he wrote for her at the bakery—all Christian has to do is sign and deliver it (not knowing that it was actually composed for Roxane). Christian resists and wants to know why Cyrano would participate. Cyrano claims that he does it to amuse himself and test his abilities.

Scene 11. The Cadets, expecting violence, open the door and find Cyrano and Christian on good terms. One takes this as a sign that Cyrano has been tamed. He insults Cyrano's nose and is knocked down. The Cadets are happy to see that Cyrano is still as brash as ever.

Act 3–Roxane's Kiss. Scene 1. In the square beneath Roxane's balcony, Ragueneau tells the duenna how his wife, Lise, left him for the musketeer and that Cyrano saved him when he tried to kill himself. He could not manage the shop alone, and so he is grateful to work now for Cyrano's cousin.

Cyrano passes by singing along with a couple of musicians that he won from a nobleman for the day. He asks Roxane about Christian. She praises Christian's intelligence, saying that it is even greater than Cyrano's. She recites lines from his letter, which she has memorized. Cyrano, the true author, basks in her praise, flattered.

De Guiche arrives. Roxane, not wanting de Guiche to find out about her affair with Christian, hides Cyrano in the house.

Scene 2. De Guiche has come to say good-bye. He is being sent to besiege the city of Arras. (France entered the Hundred Years' War in 1635. The successful siege of Arras [1640] played an important role in France's acquisition of the Artois region.) De Guiche has been promoted to colonel with command over the Cadets, Christian's (and Cyrano's) company, which has also been ordered to fight. Roxane, plotting to keep Christian from danger, convinces de Guiche that the best way to cross Cyrano is to prevent him from being sent into battle. His pride would be hurt. De Guiche, fooled into thinking that Roxane might care for him, agrees not to send the Cadets. As de Guiche leaves, Roxane warns her duenna not to tell Cyrano of her plan.

Scene 3. Roxane leaves to attend a literary gathering. She tells Cyrano that Christian should wait for her if he comes; she wants to test Christian's ability to improvise his eloquent declarations of love. Above all, Cyrano is not to prepare Christian or give him advance warning of the test. Cyrano sees Christian coming in the distance.

Scene 4. Cyrano offers to help Christian memorize what to say, but Christian refuses. He believes that Roxane now loves him and he does not need any more help. He says that he is not so unintelligent that he cannot talk of love to one who loves him, and at worst, he knows how to charm a woman physically. Cyrano leaves.

Scene 5. Roxane arrives and demands that he speak to her eloquently. Christian can only repeat that he loves her, and Roxane becomes angry. She says his inability to charm her with words is as displeasing as if he were ugly. She retreats inside her house. Cyrano returns.

Scene 6. Christian begs for Cyrano's help. Cyrano reluctantly agrees. Roxane's balcony is above. Cyrano suggests that he whisper the words to say and Christian could call them up to her, simulating improvisation. Christian throws pebbles up at the balcony to get Roxane's attention.

Scene 7. The idea works, but falters as Roxane notices the odd hesitation in Christian's voice. Cyrano, hidden in shadow, decides to speak for Christian. Roxane notices that Christian's voice has changed. Cyrano (still posing as Christian) explains that, for the first time, he is speaking his true feelings with his true voice. The irony is that these really are Cyrano's true feelings. They are interrupted when a monk arrives.

Scene 8. The monk is looking for Roxane, and Cyrano sends him away, giving him the wrong directions.

Scene 9. Christian demands that Cyrano talk Roxane into agreeing to grant him a kiss. At first Cyrano refuses but then complies, rationalizing that it is better that he win the kiss through his intellect than to have Christian win it through good looks.

Scene 10. Roxane is wooed, and Christian climbs up to kiss her. The monk returns. Cyrano pretends to arrive also and greets Roxane.

Scene 11. The monk carries a letter from de Guiche to Roxane. It indicates that instead of going into battle, he has stayed behind and is coming to see Roxane. But Roxane deceives the monk and tells him that the letter says she must marry Christian immediately. She pretends to be horrified, and the monk is convinced. She goes inside with Christian and the monk. She instructs Cyrano to wait outside and delay de Guiche.

Scene 12. Cyrano must delay de Guiche for fifteen minutes. He forms a plan and disguises himself.

Scene 13. When de Guiche arrives, Cyrano swings down on a branch from the balcony and, concealing his face with his hat, tells de Guiche that he is a man arrived from the moon. He claims there are six ways to travel to the moon. De Guiche is intrigued in spite of himself. After Cyrano reaches his sixth method, the fifteen minutes have passed, and Christian and Roxane are married. Cyrano unmasks himself.

Scene 14. De Guiche understands what has happened and takes his revenge. He reneges on his promise to Roxane to keep the Cadets from the battle and sends Christian immediately to ready them to leave. Roxane once again asks Cyrano to protect Christian; he agrees to try, but he cannot guarantee anything. She also asks that Christian write often, and Cyrano promises her that.

Act 4—The Gascon Cadets. Scene 1. At the camp outside of Arras, the men are starving. A Spanish army has besieged them and cut off their supplies. Meanwhile, Cyrano has found a way to slip through enemy lines every night to send Roxane her promised letter from "Christian." Unfortunately, he cannot carry back food because his route requires speed.

Scene 2. The starving Cadets can only think of food and are on the verge of revolt. The company commander, Carbon de Castel-Jaloux, asks Cyrano to rally them.

Scene 3. Cyrano asks an old shepherd to play some melodies from home on his pipe. Cyrano then regales them with nostalgic memories of Gascony. Carbon accuses him of making the Cadets overly homesick. Cyrano replies that it is better to cry from nostalgia than from hunger. De Guiche, although a Gascon, is not popular with the Cadets. As he arrives, Cyrano instructs the Cadets to pretend that they are not weak with hunger to save face.

Scene 4. De Guiche also shows the signs of hunger. He tells the company that he knows they do not like him. He tries to impress them with a story about his bravery on the battlefield. However, Cyrano knows that to save himself during the battle, de Guiche abandoned his white scarf, the symbol of his rank, so that he would not be marked by the enemy as a desirable target. Cyrano remarks that a true officer would not have done such a thing—that he, Cyrano, would not have dropped the scarf. When de Guiche replies that Cyrano is making an empty boast since the scarf is gone, Cyrano produces the scarf, which he had retrieved on his trip back from sending Roxane's letter.

Humiliated, de Guiche takes the scarf and uses it to signal a Spanish spy. He explains that the sign means that the Spanish will attack this spot and the Cadet defenders while the remainder of the French armies in turn attack the Spanish. The Cadets are to give their lives to allow the rest of the French army to effect the trap. He admits that he has no love for this company, that he has signed away their deaths, but that their bravery will also serve their country.

Christian knows that death might be imminent, so he wants to write Roxane a final letter. Cyrano has one ready for him. Christian reads it and notices a tear stain. Cyrano claims to have been carried away by the letter's emotion. He does not succeed in entirely convincing Christian. Fortunately for Cyrano, a carriage approaches the camp at that moment.

Scene 5. To everyone's surprise, the carriage brings Roxane. She passed through the Spanish army by smiling and claiming that she was going to visit her lover. She is urged to leave for her safety—she is warned of the battle—but she refuses. De Guiche leaves to inspect the French artillery.

Scene 6. Christian begs Roxane to leave, but she will not. The Cadets are charmed and try to tidy up. Carbon begins to introduce her to his company. He asks her for her lace handkerchief to use as their banner. Roxane reveals that she has smuggled food. Ragueneau has been her accomplice; he distributes the food to the company. They hide the food from de Guiche as he returns to the camp.

Scene 7. De Guiche has brought a cannon and now intends to stay and fight because Roxane is at the camp. Cyrano informs Christian that he has written Roxane twice every day in

Christian's name. This is much more than Christian anticipated, and he becomes enraged. He finds it very difficult to
believe that Cyrano would risk death twice daily for simple
amusement—the original reason for Cyrano's participation.

Scene 8. Roxane tells Christian that she risked the trip
here because of his letters. What is more, she says that she
really began to love him starting from the day he spoke to
her beneath her balcony in his "true" voice. She asks him to
forgive her because at first she loved him only for his beauty,
and then she loved his soul and his appearance equally, but
now she loves him for his soul alone. Christian, realizing
that the soul she describes is Cyrano's, is startled and unhappy. Roxane tries to explain that this level of love is better,
and she tells him that she would now love him even if he lost
his beauty, even if he were ugly.

Scene 9. Christian confesses to Cyrano that Roxane loves
him, Cyrano. He tells Cyrano that he knows Cyrano loves
Roxane. Cyrano admits it. Christian says that he thinks
Cyrano's looks are no longer a definite obstacle to Roxane's
love. They decide that they should tell Roxane the truth and
let her choose between them. Christian asserts that even his
marriage, secret and rushed, could be annulled, and that he
does not want Roxane if she does not really love him for himself. He calls her to them but leaves her with Cyrano alone.

Scene 10. Roxane confirms to Cyrano that she loves Christian's soul and that his looks (good or bad) would not make
a difference. Cyrano takes heart, feeling hope for the first
time, and is about to confess his feelings when Le Bret appears with news. Christian has been shot. Cyrano cannot
take what he considers unfair advantage of a man who is
about to die and resolves to never tell Roxane who the real
soul behind her letters has been. As Christian is dying,
Cyrano whispers that he has told Roxane all and that she
loves Christian. Roxane discovers a blood-stained letter on
Christian's body. It is the letter Cyrano wrote in anticipation
of their deaths. Cyrano orders de Guiche to flee and take
Roxane to safety. Those remaining engage in battle.

Act 5—Cyrano's Gazette. Scene 1. Fifteen years later, at the
Park of the Sisters of the Holy Cross in Paris, two nuns and
their superior await Cyrano's arrival. Through their discus-
sion we learn that he is poor and that he has visited Roxane
every Saturday, ever since Roxane took refuge there after
Christian's death.

Scene 2. De Guiche is now an aging duc de Grammont. He visits Roxane and asks for her forgiveness. She reveals that she keeps Christian's last letter next to her heart and that Cyrano visits every week to keep her up to date on the gossip from town. De Guiche admits to Cyrano's nobility, even as Cyrano's poverty and ill health are further revealed. He tells Le Bret that he has heard that Cyrano's life is in danger and that he should warn him. As Ragueneau appears, Roxane escorts de Guiche out.

Scene 3. Ragueneau tells Le Bret that Cyrano has had a serious accident: Someone dropped a heavy log of wood on his head as he passed underneath a window in town. They both leave to see to Cyrano. Roxane calls after them as they leave, but they do not respond.

Scene 4. Roxane is embroidering. Two sisters bring out a chair in anticipation of Cyrano's scheduled arrival and place it underneath a tree. The clock strikes the hour, and Cyrano is late. Roxane remarks how beautiful autumn is and wonders where Cyrano can be.

Scene 5. Cyrano arrives and Roxane scolds him for his tardiness—it is the first time in fourteen years that he has been late. Sister Marthe arrives and offers Cyrano some broth; she thinks he is pale from hunger. Cyrano and Roxane reflect on the falling leaves. She asks him for his usual recitation of court gossip. He begins his account but almost faints. He claims that it is his wound from Arras troubling him. Roxane says she can relate and indicates the letter over her heart. Cyrano asks to read it and as he does, Roxane recognizes the voice as the one that spoke to her under the balcony. She realizes that it is too dark for him to be actually reading the letter—he must already know it by heart. Finally, although Cyrano tries to deny it, Roxane understands that it has been Cyrano whom she has loved all this time, that it was his tears on the letter. Cyrano replies that it was Christian's blood.

Scene 6. Le Bret and Ragueneau return. They inform Roxane that Cyrano has killed himself by coming to her. Cyrano complains that even his death, caused ignobly by a piece of wood, has not been the way he would have wanted. Ragueneau reports that the dramatist Molière has stolen a scene from one of Cyrano's plays. Cyrano says that he has always been deprived of glory, forgotten, while others shine: Molière with genius and Christian with beauty. Roxane blames herself for Cyrano's unhappiness, but he contradicts her and says that she has been his one female friend. Cyrano rhapsodizes about the moon. In his final moments, he stands and makes one last speech on how he never compromised, on how, throughout everything, he always carried his panache with him.

CHAPTER 1

Creating a Comedy-Heroic

The End of the Century

Nicholas Cronk

Reaching the end of a century is often a momentous
event, triggering new attitudes and awakening old
fears. The French term *fin-de-siècle* (the end of the
century) carries these connotations. In this excerpt,
Nicholas Cronk describes the *fin-de-siècle* politics and
culture that Rostand lived and breathed while writing *Cyrano de Bergerac*. He shows how the character
of Cyrano was a revival of French nationalism and
investigates reasons behind *Cyrano's* astonishing
popularity in the theatre. Nicholas Cronk is a Fellow
and Tutor in French and Faculty Lecturer at St. Ed-
mund Hall, Oxford University. He also edited and introduced an edition of Voltaire's *Letters Concerning
the English Nation.*

The legendary Cyrano burst onto the scene with newly invented panache in 1897 when Edmond Rostand's 'heroic
comedy' *Cyrano de Bergerac* received its première to huge acclaim. What made an up-and-coming dramatist choose to
write a play about a seemingly obscure seventeenth-century
literary figure? The revival of Cyrano de Bergerac's literary
reputation had in fact begun already in the middle years of the
century. In reaction against what they saw as the excessively
rule-bound literature of French Classicism dating from the
period of Louis XIV's absolute rule (1661–1715), certain Romantic writers in the 1830s and 1840s revived interest in the
less conventional writers who had flourished in the 'pre-
classical' (and 'pre-absolutist') period. Charles Nodier and
Théophile Gautier both wrote enthusiastically about Cyrano,
and in particular it was the poet Gautier who, in an influential essay in *Les Grotesques* (1844), invented the myth of
Cyrano's long nose. An edition of Cyrano's writings published
in 1858 made his work easily available to the public for the
first time since the seventeenth century. Furthermore the

reprinting in that edition of a seventeenth-century account of Cyrano's career by his friend Le Bret gave new life to many old inaccuracies, including the false notion that Cyrano came from Bergerac in Gascony, in the south-west of France (where today there is a brisk tourist trade in postcards of Cyrano). In fact, the 'Bergerac' of his name is a small town near Paris, as was shown in a thesis on Cyrano's life and works presented at the Sorbonne in 1893 by Pierre Brun; Rostand seems not to have used Brun's work in writing his play, and anyway it suited his purposes to present Cyrano as a southerner.

AN OVERNIGHT SUCCESS

Edmond Rostand, unlike Cyrano, really was from the South of France. Born in Marseille, he went to Paris to complete his education, and it was in the capital that he began in the 1890s to make a name for himself as a dramatist and poet. The première of *Cyrano* at the Théâtre de la Porte-Saint-Martin in Paris on 28 December 1897 was a sensational success which has become part of French theatrical legend. It transformed Rostand, overnight, into the leading French literary celebrity of the day; within two months of the first night, Toulouse-Lautrec had produced a lithograph of Coquelin *aîné* in the role of Cyrano. Coquelin and Sarah Bernhardt performed the play in New York in 1900, and the following year in London (though Bernhardt never performed the role of Roxane in France). And in 1901, when still only in his early thirties, Rostand was elected to the Académie française. He went on to write several other works for the stage, notably *L'Aiglon,* and *Chantecler,* which is sometimes considered his best work. But he was never able to repeat the popular success of *Cyrano.* When Rostand died, just three weeks after the end of the First World War, it was for *Cyrano* that he was remembered. The early reception of the play was phenomenal: it reached its thousandth Paris performance in 1913, and it has been estimated that in that one year alone there were altogether 3,000 performances in France.

No other French play in the period enjoyed anything like this success with the public: *Cyrano* evidently touched a chord in the audience of the time, and to understand the play's unprecedented impact we need to look more closely at the state of France in the 1880s and 1890s, the period which the French themselves dubbed the *fin-de-siècle.* France achieved national unity far later than is generally supposed, and the need to forge a national identity was still keenly felt at the turn of the century [as historian Eugen Weber notes in his book *Peasants into Frenchmen*]:

> Despite evidence to the contrary, inhabitants of the hexagon in 1870 generally knew themselves to be French subjects, but to many this status was no more than an abstraction. The people of whole regions felt little identity with the state or with people of other regions. Before this changed, before the inhabitants of France could come to feel a significant community, they had to share significant experiences with each other. Roads, railroads, schools, markets, military service, and the circulation of money, goods, and printed matter provided those experiences, swept away old commitments, instilled a national view of things in regional minds, and confirmed the power of that view by offering advancement to those who adopted it. The national ideology was still diffuse and amorphous around the middle of the nineteenth century. French culture became truly national only in the last years of the century.

Cyrano is certainly a celebration of France and of Frenchness; and the symbolism is all the more powerful because Cyrano is depicted as a Gascon, a southerner, fighting for the glory of the French nation as a whole. Cyrano and his fellow soldiers are suspicious of the power and pretensions of the Comte de Guiche: but when in Act IV the Comte's accent slips and he reveals himself as a man of the Midi, all are reconciled.

A CHANGING WORLD

Another feature of the *fin-de-siècle* is bewilderment at the speed of change. Charles Péguy, a poet of peasant stock, wrote in *L'Argent* (1913) that the world had changed more since his school-days in the 1880s than it had changed from the time of the Romans to the 1880s. The telegraph, the telephone, the typewriter, the electric light, the lift, the bicycle, the tram, the Métro are all innovations of the *fin-de-siècle*, and some, like the bicycle, were advertised in the vivacious and highly coloured posters which are so characteristic of Paris at this time. Yet notwithstanding the real improvement in living standards experienced by large parts of the population, the *fin-de-siècle* saw itself as a period of moral and artistic decadence. The material progress constituted by these new inventions 'may have helped palliate the shortcomings of the political class,' writes Eugen Weber [in his book *France, Fin de Siècle*], 'but they disturbed the more austere who feared for the national fibre'.

Cyrano's swashbuckling courage and ticklish sense of honour might seem out of place in this world of typewriters and bicycles; but the aristocratic ethos of personal honour survived with surprising persistence in the bourgeoisie of the Third Republic—it has been estimated that there were as many as 300 duels a year in France in the 1880s and 1890s, many of them involving journalists, writers, and politicians. Cyrano's penchant for flamboyant duelling takes on a new colouring when we recall that the Radical politician Georges Clemenceau, nicknamed 'the Tiger', fought twenty-two duels in his career, all of them widely reported in the press; a restaurant on the Grande Jatte outside Paris was a favoured rendezvous of duellists, and its owner claimed that Clemenceau booked an average of three duels a week. So when de Guiche tells the Gascon cadets fighting for France at the siege of Arras 'You are all unrivalled in courage', he speaks directly to the concerns of the *fin-de-siècle* [as historian Robert Nye explains in his book *Masculinity and Male Codes of Honor in Modern France*].

> In the context of military crisis and fear of national decline that reigned in France in the period 1890–1914, courage was a universally prized quality . . . Because the French lagged behind Germany in both material resources and population, they were obliged to compensate for this deficit by developing superior 'spiritual' qualities, of which courage was perhaps the most important . . . One is able to find considerable evidence of a self-conscious social effort to cultivate the noble flowers of courage and heroism and eradicate the weeds of cowardice and fear that inhibited their growth.

TROUBLED TIMES

The Third Republic could never forget that it had come into being with the Prussian invasion of France in 1870, and although by the 1890s the Republic seemed to be established, the political scene was none the less turbulent. Memories of the humiliation of the Franco-Prussian War were still keen—when *Lohengrin* was performed in Paris in 1891 (the first Wagner production by the Opéra since 1861), the police had to be called in to quell the riots. In the years 1887–9, General Boulanger and his supporters had come close to overthrowing the Republic, and the Panama scandal of 1892, a financial scandal which affected prominent politicans including Clemenceau, provoked further unrest. The Socialist movement was growing, and in the years 1892–4 there were a series of anarchist explosions in Paris; then in 1894 President Carnot was stabbed to death in Lyon by an Italian anarchist. The anarchist movement made a deep impression on French culture in the 1890s, affecting literature and the visual arts as much as politics. The Republic appeared to have lost its way, and a succession of moderate governments struggled in vain to calm the crisis.

It was against this background of instability that the Dreyfus Affair erupted. In 1894, Captain Alfred Dreyfus, a Jewish army officer, was found guilty of spying for the Germans, and sentenced to deportation to Devil's Island; new evidence subsequently invalidated the court martial's verdict, but the army, supported by the government, sought to suppress it. The existence of this evidence became publicly known in late 1897, so that the Affair had reached a point of crisis just at the moment of the première of *Cyrano*. Less than a fortnight after the triumphant first night, on 10 January 1898, Major Esterhazy, the true spy, was acquitted by a court martial, prompting Émile Zola, three days later, to publish his article '*J'Accuse*', an open letter to the President, Félix Faure (who only a week earlier had attended with his family a performance of *Cyrano*). 'From Zola's manifesto,' writes [historian] John McManners, 'France was riven by a moral cataclysm.' The nation was split into two warring camps, the *Dreyfusards*, who demanded a retrial for Dreyfus, and the anti-*Dreyfusards*, who stood by the original verdict, and who, against all the evidence, supported Army and Church. This became the defining issue dividing Left and Right, creating a split which brought to a head all manner of tensions in the Third Republic: monarchist versus republican, Catholic versus Protestant/Jew/Freemason, army versus antimilitarist. It was to have long-lasting political repercussions, most notably the legal separation of Church and State in 1905; in the short term, the Republic was further destabilized, and when President Faure died in 1899 (not at the hands of an anarchist but in the arms of his mistress), his funeral became the occasion for an attempted *coup d'état* which farcically demonstrated the fragility of the regime.

The leading authors of the day were prominent in these political debates, and indeed the Affair played a pivotal role in defining the modern French notion of the literary intellectual; Zola, Proust, and Anatole France were among the *Dreyfusards*, while the opposing camp included Claudel and Valéry. Rostand was also a *Dreyfusard* but, like Gide (who was a year his junior), he did not adopt a high profile in the Affair, and his sympathy for the cause of Dreyfus does not appear to have alienated his potential audience—on the contrary, the extraordinary reception given to the play suggests that *Cyrano* appealed to audiences across the divide opened up by the Dreyfus Affair. In a political atmosphere which was so tense, every detail of the play could be politically charged (and not least, in this climate of rabid anti-Semitism, the possession of an oversize nose). On the one hand, the play offers us the comforting image of a brave and fearless soldier who hails from a golden age of French military might; on the other hand, Cyrano is an anti-establishment figure, fiercely independent, who relishes challenging authority. One explanation for the phenomenal early success of *Cyrano* is that it spoke to all Frenchmen and united them as few other works of the period could have done.

THE THRIVING THEATRE

If this was a time of political turbulence, it was a period of artistic challenge too, the era of Symbolism and *fin-de-siècle* Decadence, when the avant-garde was provoking a powerful conservative backlash. It was only in February 1897, for example, after a prolonged battle, that the first Impressionist paintings were publicly displayed, in the musée du Luxembourg. Of all the art forms, it was theatre which, in Paris at least, was the most popular and the most diverse. A journalist of the time observed that 'the population of Paris lives in the theatre, for the theatre, by the theatre', and it has been estimated that in the 1880s and 1890s half a million Parisians visited the theatre once a week, and more than twice that number once a month.

The plays that they flocked to see were not, by and large, the plays dwelt on at length in the literary histories. Alfred-Jarry's *Ubu-Roi* (1896) played for just one performance, and Maurice Maeterlinck's *Pelléas et Mélisande* (1892) is remembered now largely on account of Debussy's opera (1902). While the Paris premières of Ibsen, Strindberg, and Hauptmann played for short runs in small theatres (not always with success—during performances of Ibsen's *Wild Duck*, sections of the public took to quacking at inopportune moments), the masses flocked to see highly spectacular productions of melodramas, fairy-tales, and adventure stories. Rostand's great achievement with *Cyrano* was to write a play which defied easy categorization, a drama which was neither modern nor traditional, and yet both at the same time. The seventeenth-century setting evokes the period of France's military and political supremacy; yet this vision of the Age of Richelieu also evokes an earlier nineteenth-century treatment of the period, [Alexandre] Dumas's *The Three Musketeers* (1844)—it is a nice touch that d'Artagnan should meet Cyrano fleetingly in the first act.

Rostand's choice of subject remains, however, a surprising one. It was during the last years of the century that literary history was 'invented' as a scientific discipline, as exemplified in Gustave Lanson's monumental *Histoire de la littérature française* (1895). The school and university syllabuses of the Third Republic, influenced by the new literary histories, gave canonical status to seventeenth-century French Classicism. Lanson's seventeenth century is the Age of the Sun King, an era of religious and political orthodoxy; the free-thinking, distinctly unorthodox Cyrano de Bergerac hardly fits into this view of the *grand siècle*, so Lanson's *Histoire* consigns him to a footnote. It is a pleasing paradox, and a tribute to Rostand's knowledge of the seventeenth century, that his wilfully inaccurate and anachronistic play did more to restore the literary fortunes of Cyrano de Bergerac than all the positivistic literary criticism of the Sorbonne professors.

THE OLD MADE NEW

Written in five acts and in alexandrine (twelve-syllable) rhyming couplets, Rostand's play mimics the form of seventeenth-century classical theatre, an example of which he incorporates into the opening act (in imitation of Molière's *L'Impromptu de Versailles*); but again, the classicism is more apparent than real. Rostand did not repeat the mistake made by the librettists of Massenet's opera *Le Cid* (1885), Édouard Blau and Louis Gallet, who incorporated into their libretto lines lifted directly from Corneille's drama; this attempt at authenticity produced only oddness, partly because alexandrines are difficult to set to music, but partly also because a poetic language ripped from its context loses its dramatic cogency. Rostand well understood one of the key principles of French classical poetics, that what is plausible (*vraisemblable*) matters more than what is true (*vrai*): his alexandrines sound authentic precisely because they are not. A parallel may be found in the most characteristic artistic expression of these years, *Art Nouveau.* This style, though unquestionably new, was explicitly inspired by the principles of the rococo; it was a means by which the grace and elegance of the Louis XV interior could be recreated in the decade following the construction of the Eiffel Tower (1889). Rostand, for his part, creates a dramatic *Art Nouveau,* evoking an older style with all its connotations of tradition and charm, while in fact creating something entirely original.

Separating Man
from Myth

Geoffrey Strachan

An air of mystery often colors reports concerning the
real Savinien Cyrano (later to call himself Cyrano de
Bergerac). Because of his sometimes controversial
activities, descriptions of his life have been simulta-
neously censored and elaborated. This confusion existed before Rostand wrote his famous play, but
Cyrano de Bergerac's publication amplified the problem. Geoffrey Strachan takes on the imposing task of
sifting through fact and fiction to find the truth behind the Cyrano legend. His Cyrano is also a writer,
but one who is often more human than heroic. Geoffrey Strachan has translated Cyrano de Bergerac's
L'Autre Monde [Other Worlds] and won the 1998
Times Literary Supplement-Scott Moncrieff Prize for
his translation of Andrei Makine's *Le Testament
Français* [Dreams of My Russian Summers].

Visitors to the town of Bergerac on the Dordogne [a river of SW
France] can buy picture postcards which show a man in a
plumed hat with a bulbous upturned nose. The caption reads:
'Cyrano de Bergerac, legendary hero'. In such ways the name of
a gifted and influential seventeenth-century French writer—
who happened to have a prominent aquiline nose—has been di-
vorced from historical reality; the man who three hundred years
ago portrayed the hazards of space flight in two brilliant novels
still has to compete for its use with the soft-centred fictional
hero of a late nineteenth-century box office smash hit.
 ' Little is known for certain about the life of Savinien Cyrano
de Bergerac. Even the reports of his friends contribute as
much to legend as to history—he emerges too sober or too in-
temperate. He was born Savinien Cyrano in Paris in 1619, the
son of an *avocat au Parlement de Paris* [Parisian parliamen-
tary lawyer], named Abel de Cyrano. Three years later, the

Excerpted from the Introduction, by Geoffrey Strachan, © 1965 by Geoffrey Strachan,
to *Other Worlds*, by Cyrano de Bergerac, translated by Geoffrey Strachan (London: Oxford University Press, 1965). Reprinted by permission of Geoffrey Strachan.

family moved to their estate near Paris, part of which was the small fief of Bergerac. Savinien was educated first by a country priest, whose punishments made him resentful and rebellious. At the age of thirteen, he was sent by his father to the Collège de Beauvais in Paris, but not before he had met at school his lifelong friend and future literary executor, Henri Le Bret. At the Collège de Beauvais, the young Savinien studied his classics and fell foul of the principal, Jean Grangier, a classical scholar of some standing, but apparently himself of a quarrelsome disposition and a fierce disciplinarian. His various weaknesses, real and imaginary, were later outrageously burlesqued in Cyrano's comedy, *Le Pédant Joué*. In 1636 Abel sold his property at Bergerac and the family moved to Paris once more, but Savinien was to adopt the name of Bergerac and to use it throughout his life in various forms: Alexandre de Cyrano Bergerac, de Bergerac Cyrano, Hercule de Bergerac and the more familiar Cyrano de Bergerac.

At about eighteen, he left the Collège de Beauvais, having doubtless acquired a considerable humanist culture, as well as a deep dislike of arbitrary authority. He mixed with the literary bohemian world of the period, which included such people as François Tristan L'Hermite, the playwright. He frequented taverns and indulged in gambling, a pastime his father's fortunes could ill afford. He probably also read widely and voraciously. Henri Le Bret remained his friend and adviser and something of a mediator between Cyrano and his father. It was on Le Bret's suggestion that he enlisted with M. de Carbon de Casteljaloux's company of guards, his admission being facilitated by the noble and Gascon ring of his new name, for both qualifications were required in this company. He was apparently soon involved in many duels and acquitted himself well. He is said to have fought only as a second (the normal custom for seconds then) and never in his own quarrels. He received a musket shot through the body at the siege of Mouzon in Champagne in the bitter winter of 1639, and the following year he was again wounded, this time at Arras and in the throat. Soon after this he abandoned his military career, with a weakened constitution but having won considerable respect from his brother officers.

Back to Civilian Life

In 1641 he returned to a life of study at the Collège de Lisieux, perhaps earning his keep as an usher. He attended the classes of Gassendi, the Epicurean philosopher, mathematician and free-thinker, newly arrived in Paris. His pupils included brilliant young men of Cyrano's generation like Molière and Jacques Rohault, the disciple of Descartes, who was to remain a close friend of Cyrano and to guide him in his study of physics.

A number of stories are told about his exploits at this period. Those told by Le Bret (which include routing a band of a hundred hired ruffians in order to protect the poet Lignières) do him credit. Others indicate a preposterously vain and ill-tempered disposition and belong to the burlesque legend built up by less loyal friends, such as the poet Charles

---

ROSTAND'S INSPIRATION

In Cyrano de Bergerac, *Edmond Rostand created a character born of fact, myth, and his own imagination.*

When Rostand was asked if his interest in Cyrano de Bergerac had begun in his childhood, he replied: "Yes and no; I was for a long time pursued by that personage Cyrano; he haunted me at College and gradually, with some help from me, he became the center of a dramatic action." In this same conversation, recently published by his intimate neighbor at Cambo, Paul Faure, Rostand traced the growth of this early interest toward the finished play. In school he had come greatly to admire a master "whose soul was as beautiful as his body was ugly." The final incentive to make a play on the theme came from Rostand's own assumption of the part in real life. He shared the love secrets of a dull and bashful schoolmate who had failed to make any progress with an evasive young lady. Rostand spurred him on and finally dictated love letters that won not only the girl but also the boy's father—who had artfully intercepted them—to a belief in the young rascal's genius. Even the duel, which to most readers no doubt passes as the good old stuff of footlights and laths, was for Rostand the vivid revival of another boyhood memory, that of a man who fought a duel while visiting Edmond's father and who allowed the young poet to play with the swords. The final composition of the play, as was true of all he wrote, was long delayed and painstakingly elaborated. For years he was "afraid to touch it," and the writing itself was "a kind of torture with constant change and rewriting and replanning." In later years ill health still further extended the time of writing.

E. Bradlee Watson and Benfield Pressey, eds., *Contemporary Drama*. New York: Charles Scribner's Sons, 1941.

Dassoucy, with whom at times he quarrelled. It seems certain that Cyrano mixed intelligent conversation and studies with a fairly dissolute way of life, during which he gambled with Tristan L'Hermite, contracted syphilis, which was never properly cured, helped to impoverish his father, broadened his knowledge of current scientific and philosophical ideas, talked well, and wrote his comedy, *Le Pédant Joué,* from which Molière was to borrow heavily for one of the most famous scenes in *Les Fourberies de Scapin* (1671). He began to write the literary letters later collected together as *Lettres Diverses, Lettres Satiriques* and *Lettres Amoureuses,* exercises in elegance, wit, and invective. He may have travelled at this time to England, Italy, and Poland, where some say he observed experiments with a flying machine, a winged dragon that beat its wings. In 1648 he first appeared in print with a preface to one of Dassoucy's poems.

EARLY SCIENCE FICTION

About this time, Le Bret tells us, Cyrano refused the offered patronage of the Maréchal de Gassion—because he wished to remain a free man. He was for the moment somewhat less impoverished, as a result of the death of his father, whom he and his brother, Abel, are alleged to have robbed as he lay dying. He now began to work on *L'Autre Monde* (literally, 'The Other World'). In 1648 there had been published a French edition of Bishop Godwin's *The Man in the Moone,* the fanciful tale of one Domingo Gonsales, who was carried to the moon on a machine borne by a number of large birds. Once in the moon, he made a study of its utopian institutions. The French edition is prefaced by the remarks: 'If, reader, you have ever seen either the *True History* of Lucian, or Thomas More's *Utopia,* or Chancellor Bacon's *New Atlantis,* I have no doubt that you will class with the same type of writing this story, which is no less ingenious than diverting.' Cyrano would know these books, as well as Campanella's rationalist utopia, *The City of the Sun,* and perhaps Kepler's fragmentary *Somnium,* a tale of a trip to the moon. This was envisaged in quite realistic terms, with a light face and a dark face to the moon, and a race of huge reptiles living there. Cyrano's own book was to be broader in scope than any of these.

In 1649 he ventured into print again with a 'mazarinade', an unbridled attack on Mazarin in the manner of the burlesque poets like [Paul] Scarron. The following year he changed sides and wrote (either for money, or to spite Scarron and the rest) his letter, *Contre les Frondeurs,* an attack on the princes of the Fronde. Meanwhile *L'Autre Monde* (or at any rate the first book of it) was completed. He sent the manuscript of it to his friend, the poet Jean Royer de Prades, who expressed in verse his alarm and his intention of avoiding Cyrano in future:

> Car autant qu'une affreuse mort
> Je crains les gens de 'L'Autre Monde'.

(I fear these people of 'The Other World' as greatly as a dreadful death.) The reaction of other friends is unknown. The manuscript remained unpublished, though its private circulation probably added to his reputation both as a writer and as a dangerous *libertin* (i.e. a free-thinker). What the text of this first book, *The States and Empires of the Moon* (or *Voyage in the Moon*) and its sequel, *The History* show is a brilliant narrative invention and a sceptical spirit that mark Cyrano as a forerunner of Voltaire and Montesquieu, challenging the astronomical orthodoxy imposed by the Catholic Church, which discouraged the notion that the moon could be a planet, a world, like earth, or that the sun might be the centre of the universe. Both books, published after his death in somewhat bowdlerized form, achieved considerable success and ran into several editions. They were twice translated into English, influenced Swift's *Gulliver's Travels,* surfaced again in the mid-nineteenth century and have been reissued in four separate editions in France in the past fifty years. Modern readers of Act III scenes XIII and XIV in Rostand's play *Cyrano de Bergerac,* in which his hero apparently improvises several methods of travelling to the moon, may be interested to know that these inventions were mainly lifted from the real Cyrano's own texts, two minor classics of early science fiction, whose author was arguably a man of more intellectual substance than Rostand's romantic fictional creation.

STIRRING UP CONTROVERSY

In 1652 Cyrano overcame any earlier scruples, driven perhaps both by poverty and by the need for respectability, which would permit him to publish, and obtained the patronage of the dull and vain Duc d'Arpajon. His tragedy, *La Mort d'Agrippine,* was published with a dedication to his new patron and this was fol-

lowed by a second volume of works, including *Le Pèdant Joué.*
L'Autre Monde remained unpublished, but the audience which
witnessed the first performance of *La Mort d'Agrippine* at the
Hotel de Bourgogne evidently came prepared to be shocked
by the work of a madman or an atheist or both. Bold tirades
against the gods ('which were made by man and did not
make man') may have passed unnoticed but a harmless
phrase was taken as an insult to the Eucharist (*hostie* can
mean both victim and the Host) and an uproar ensued. The
play was taken off and the duke sought to rid himself of his
embarrassing protégé.

But by this time, fate (or as some biographers have had it,
the agents of the Holy Office) had intervened and caused a
wooden beam to fall on Cyrano's head as he entered the
duke's house. He was now ill and confined to his room. The
duke advised him to go to the country. Feeling betrayed,
Cyrano left the duke's house for good, and was tended by his
aunt, Catherine, and his friends at a house in Paris. Here he
worked over the manuscripts of *L'Autre Monde* until they
were stolen—or removed by friends in order to save them
from destruction at the hands of the pious nuns, who were
also in attendance. They later came into the hands of Le
Bret, but he, in turn, was robbed of the third book, *L'Étincelle,*
which has never come to light. Cyrano moved to the house
of his cousin, Pierre de Cyrano at Sannois, where he died in
July 1655, at the age of thirty-six, probably of the malady
which had kept him away from the opposite sex for the last
ten years of his life. Apparently he made a Christian end. If
there was a tragic element in Cyrano's life—apart from his
premature death—it was surely that he was born a century
too soon: his questing spirit would have been more at home
in the eighteenth century, the century of the *philosophes* and
the *encyclopédistes.* The tragedy of having an ugly face is not
a theme that occurs in Cyrano's own work and belongs very
much with the nineteenth-century obsession with the
grotesque, as famously evinced in the work of E.T.A. Hoff-
man and Rostand himself.[1]

1. Theophile Gautier in a highly inaccurate account in *Les Grotesques* (1844) penned
a whimsical description of Cyrano's face, based on the extant portraits. It is vivid and
exaggerated. His surprising description of Cyrano's big aquiline nose as 'the highest
mountain in the world after the Himalayas' helped . . . to lay the foundations for Rostand's creation.

A Virtuoso Play

Harold R. Walley

Harold R. Walley defines a virtuoso play as one that
is tailored to showcase the talent of a specific actor.
According to Walley, this type of play is often entertaining because of the standout performance but offers little in the way of genuine novelty or artistic
achievement. For these reasons, virtuoso plays usually receive criticism for being clever, but not brilliant. Some critics have categorized *Cyrano de Bergerac* as a virtuoso play because Rostand created the
role of Cyrano with the famous French actor Benoît
Constant Coquelin in mind. In this excerpt, however,
Walley notes that *Cyrano de Bergerac* is unique
among virtuoso plays. Though derivative and thoroughly conventional, Rostand's play is so technically
and stylistically perfect that it persuades audiences
to forgive its conventionality and partake of its illu-
sory world. Harold R. Walley was a professor of English at Ohio State University and wrote books related to the study of the theater, including *Early
Seventeenth-Century Plays, 1600–1642.*

No survey of dramatic achievement can be complete without
some attention to its most common, if least memorable,
manifestation. This category of drama, unlike the others dis-
cussed earlier, is not distinguished by any special features of
form or technique; parasitically it uses any established type
of drama as its host. Its unique character is simply a product
of its underlying purpose. For lack of a more generally accepted name, it may be described as virtuoso drama. The nature of this particular phenomenon is attributable to a pecu-
liarity of art itself. In general, the development of any art
may be said to represent an evolution from ritual toward virtuosity. That is to say, art begins as a functional adjunct to
the process of living, often in connection with religious or

magical practices; as it develops it evolves an increasingly elaborate and refined technique, the skill and effectiveness of which are capable of affording an increment of aesthetic pleasure; and it culminates in such a proficiency and sub-tlety of technique that the very exercise of it constitutes its own aesthetic justification. In other words, the inevitable trend of the process is from art for life's sake toward art for art's sake. From this trend derives a common duality in artistic achievement. For example, in the realm of music, a composer may draw upon all the resources of an orchestra to give substance to an important musical conception; on the other hand, he may deliberately contrive a musical compo-sition for the sake of entertaining with an ingenious display of his own technical facility, the possibilities of the instru-ments, and the virtuosity of the performers. As employments of genuine art, both are eminently legitimate and enjoyable; but in their ultimate value there is a vast difference. The first provides a significant human experience; the second, a mo-mentarily exhilarating diversion. Virtuoso drama is the the-atrical version of this second artistic category.

What Is Good Theater?

Every successful play is a product of skilled craftsmanship. Whatever its final intention or value, its artistic achievement is a matter of calculated theatrical effect. What is known as "good theater," therefore, is an essential element of all dra-matic art. Moreover, good theater remains good theater re-gardless of the uses to which it is put; for one's response to skilfully contrived theatrical effects and the immediate sat-isfaction one derives from them have very little to do with their inherent justification. For this reason it is possible to divorce good theater from significant drama and still retain a quite acceptable form of entertainment. One is not refer-ring here to specious and pretentious drama, which is sim-ply an example of bad dramatic art; for pretentious profes-sion of what is never intended is intellectually and artistically as meretricious in the theater as in life. Dramatic virtuosity is an entirely different affair. As a business enter-prise and an entertainment facility, the theater has always been a wholesale dispenser of this commodity; nor is there anything especially reprehensible about the practice. Pre-tending to be no more than it is, at its best it affords an in-nocuous and quite legitimate delight in artistic dexterity, and at its worst it is no worse than an amiable method of killing time. In dealing with a play of this sort, however, it is always advisable to bear in mind one important characteristic: while it does not necessarily present "a tale told by an idiot," it is by nature largely "full of sound and fury, signifying nothing," or, at most, not very much.

CLEVER BUT SUPERFICIAL

All serious dramatic art, whether tragic or comic, involves a basic relationship between drama and life; that is, there is always an inherent correlation between what it presents on the stage and the actualities of human experience, so that its creation of theatrical effects is always a means to a larger end. In contrast, the most distinctive feature of the virtuoso play is its exclusive theatricality. The production of amusing or sensational effects is its sole concern. Not only are these effects regarded as a sufficient end in themselves, but they constitute the whole reason for the play's existence. Removed from their immediate impact, the play becomes a bloodless phantom. Designed as strictly a theater piece, it is a performance calculated in terms of production opportunities. Its situations are contrived of factitious artifices to create a predetermined effect; its characters are conceived histrionically; its criterion of artistic excellence is the successfully manipulated *coup de théâtre*. Whereas serious drama strives for an effect which is appropriate to the circumstances with which it deals, the virtuoso play reverses the process; beginning with a desirable effect, it works backward to a mechanical pretext for producing it. Because of this subordination of cause to effect, it is inevitably more concerned with sensations and sentiments than with reality or authentic emotion. Correspondingly its chief virtue is not revelation of truth but the clever ingenuity with which it contrives artful impressions. Superficial as mere mechanical dexterity and momentary brilliance may be, within their limitations they are none the less capable of a considerable novelty, suspense, excitement, and sentimental pleasure. Their greatest liability is their ephemerality. Not only do such superficial appeals by nature lack the substance necessary to sustain them beyond their appointed theatrical moment, but where no great value is at stake, replacement is cheap. The result is that plays of this sort are notoriously short lived. Having served their purpose of transitory enjoyment, they are readily supplanted by fresh competitors, no better in their kind, but with the advantage of novelty and more immediate interest.

One of the most conspicuous exceptions thus far to this rule is the so-called heroic comedy *Cyrano de Bergerac*, by the French dramatist Edmond Rostand (1868–1918). Something of an international sensation when it first appeared in 1897, the play has enjoyed in several versions, both on the stage and in print, a sustained success and durability which are by way of making it a modern classic of its genre. The tremendous success of the play, its unquestionable dramatic effectiveness, its appealing idealism, and its sensitive poetic expression, however, do not alter the fact that it is fundamentally a masterpiece of theatrical virtuosity. As a matter of fact, it is a veritable mosaic of tested devices, infallible situations, sanctified conventions, well-worn themes, stereotyped sentiments, and approved stylistic artifices. In its inception it was deliberately designed as a vehicle to exploit the versatile talents of the celebrated French actor Constant Coquelin. From beginning to end it is skilfully contrived to exhibit a fascinating personality in a variety of piquant situations. In the process the whole storehouse of theatrical tradition is ransacked to furnish situations of demonstrated effectiveness, characters of certified interest, and sentiments of guaranteed appeal. The historical subject matter is chosen for its glamor and quaintness. The settings are ostentatiously picturesque. Characters are tailormade to standard romantic measurements. Incidents are prefabricated to provide a dazzling array of gallant feats, stirring crises, noble gestures, tender moments, witty exchanges, and bravura rhapsodies. Spectacle follows on spectacle, and each act brings down the curtain on a stunning tableau. With a masterly touch on the strings of human susceptibility, the play runs the whole gamut of heroic valor, exalted passion, impudent gayety, astringent wit, graceful sentiment, idyllic yearning, tender compassion, and ironic pathos. Everything is deliberately calculated; every scene, every speech, every gesture is expertly contrived, but with such impeccable style and such exquisite theatrical finesse that, under the spell of its illusion, one is ready to swear it the very stuff of life. Yet a moment's more sober reflection will testify that it is actually as false and factitious as the nose without which no actor could possibly be Cyrano. It is a fabric manufactured of whole cloth—a tissue of magnificent artifice, conceived in the essential spirit of Cyrano himself, and dedicated to the principle which Cyrano has so admirably expressed— "what a gesture!"

The virtues of such a play are those of a luxurious motor-car or any other piece of fine machinery. They afford pleasure by their smooth efficiency, sleek beauty, and capacity to minister to one's comfort and civilized enjoyment. They serve their purpose so admirably because they are features built in to satisfy the customer. For touring pleasure, what is more engaging than picturesque terrain and glamorous inhabitants? For ease, pick-up, and smooth performance, what more reassuring than gallant spirit, agile wit, and dashing valor? For relaxed comfort, what more delightful than love, especially hapless and deathless love, designed with exquisite sentiment and trimmed in impassioned eloquence? And for sheer power when needed, what more satisfying than heroic honor with over-drive of impregnable integrity and noble renunciation? These custom-built appointments there is no effort to conceal; on the contrary, awareness of them is designed to add to the customer's pleasure. One misses the whole brilliance of Rostand's virtuosity unless one recognizes the delicate balance of wit and sentiment, the intricate counterpoint of humor and heroics, the adroit manipulation of suspense, reversal of situation, parallelism and contrast of themes, preparation of theatrical effects, and timing of surprise. The fact that these features are strictly machine-made, are quite unnatural, and coincide with the probabilities of neither reality nor romance has nothing whatever to do with the case. Their justification is their immediate theatrical effectiveness. Their art is the magical virtuosity with which they enchant the passing moment.

AN ILLUSION OF REALITY

The ability to perform this feat calls attention to a curious factor in drama, without which the virtuoso play would lose most of its effectiveness. On the face of it, there is scarcely a scene in *Cyrano de Bergerac* which is not highly implausible. The duel of the ballade, the celebrated balcony scene, the ebbing of Cyrano's life in a symbolic autumn twilight, with the leaves falling and the light fading, to one last white plume of expiring defiance—these are figments of the artistic fancy rather than probabilities of any human experience.

As for the gaudy events of the climactic fourth act, they are not only incredible but patently preposterous. Yet no play can possibly capture the imagination of an audience unless it creates an illusion of some kind of reality. To this inexorable law the play of theatrical virtuosity is as much subject as any other drama. The reality which it seeks in its illusion, however, is based not on human existence, whether conceived realistically or romantically, objectively or subjectively, but on life as it exists in the theater. For the curious fact is that the theater actually does possess a life of its own, different in many respects from that beyond its doors, but amazingly comprehensive and sufficient unto itself. As drama is the creator of this life, to a certain extent all drama is also its creature. Being entirely a product of it, the drama of pure artifice owes its whole effectiveness to its expression of this theatrical reality.

As the basis of all theatrical art is the will to make believe, the reality of every theatrical illusion is to a greater or less extent the reality of make-believe. Now, make-believe is simply a process of asserting that things are so because it is convenient that they should be so. The end result is the only relevant consideration, and the only requisite is that matters be understood. Without this initial profession of faith the world of theatrical art could not exist. Nevertheless, theatrical belief is by no means the same as simple credulity, nor is the world which it creates a haphazard one. Its conventions of make-believe are quite systematic and orderly; they are the product of practical expediency; and in their operation they exercise the force of logical law. By a process of trial and error the theater has hit upon its own way of arranging human affairs plausibly, agreeably, and artistically. It has identified situations which may be considered properly dramatic, codified human motives, stereotyped modes of speaking and acting, and prescribed the methods by which it is to be interpreted. By adapting the materials of life to the exigencies of art it has evolved an ordered and rationalized form of existence in which the distinction between truth and accepted pretense has become increasingly tenuous. The inherent conservatism of dramatic art and its tenacity of precedent have further consolidated this material into a continuing body of established principles and practices. The result is that over the centuries the theater has accumulated a heritage of tradition and convention which amounts in effect to an independent record of human experience. While in many respects this theatrical pageant parallels the course of actual life, there are also important differences; for men do not always behave the same on the stage as in the street, nor do events fall out in exactly the same way. For purposes of dramatic plausibility, however, the sanction of theatrical precedent is often quite as persuasive as the testimony of life. It is upon this traditional life of the theater that a play like *Cyrano de Bergerac* bases its illusion of reality, and it is from the accumulated sanction of this theatrical reality that it derives its momentary semblance of truth.

CHAPTER 2

Major Themes

READINGS ON
CYRANO DE BERGERAC

Beauty and the Beast

Charles Marowitz

Studying a work's major themes helps develop understanding of an author's intent and the quality of the work. With the inclusion of a beautiful maiden loved by a noble—but not traditionally handsome—hero, *Cyrano de Bergerac*'s main characters form a classic example of the "Beauty and the Beast" theme. These elements are well-suited to a good, ill-fated romance, but is the material too lightweight for a classic play? In this critique, Charles Marowitz gives his take on Rostand's literary relevance and addresses the use of the folktale motif. Charles Marowitz has adapted and translated many plays, including Smith and Kraus's English version of *Cyrano de Bergerac*. Marowitz's other works include a radical series of Shakespeare adaptations, *The Marowitz Shakespeare.* He has also been the lead critic for the *LA Herald Examiner* and the West Coast Theater Critic for *Theater Week Magazine.*

Like most adolescents of my period, I fell in love with *Cyrano de Bergerac* around the time I started high school. The love affair was consummated when the Stanley Kramer film starring Jose Ferrer appeared, making concrete the fanciful longings stirred by the text.

When I reached the age of discretion, I thought back to *Cyrano* as one would a teenage romance which, though largely an infatuation, still left indelible marks. As one became aware of the riches of Shakespeare and Marlowe, Dryden and Webster, Edmond Rostand's talent became, in retrospect, brittle, even negligible. Later on however, after one had become somewhat weighed down with the heavyweight classics, one returned with a renewed appreciation for the simpler pleasures of works like *Cyrano.* In one's maturity, it became clear that art, like food, had different densities—and

Excerpted from the Introduction, by Charles Marowitz, © 1995 by Charles Marowitz, to *Cyrano de Bergerac*, by Edmond Rostand, translated by Charles Marowitz (Lyme, NH: Smith and Kraus, 1995). Reprinted by permission of Charles Marowitz.

sometimes a burger and a milkshake were preferable to a four course meal and provided a gastronomic high of an entirely different order.

It is Edmond Rostand's curse that one always begins by qualifying his talent and apologizing for his work—as if liking Rostand was tantamount to culturally slumming. This is an impulse that never arises when watching his play but seems to be unavoidable in critical evaluations. Therefore, let me say at the outset that, just as [Robert] Herrick and [Thomas] Campion [17th century English poets] need suffer no sense of inferiority when compared to Shakespeare and [Christopher] Marlowe, so there is no need for us to justify our liking for Rostand. In fact, to put things into a proper perspective, *Cyrano de Bergerac* is a far sturdier piece of craftsmanship than *Pericles* or *The Siege at Rhodes*, confirmed by the fact that it has not been out of the modern repertoire since its first production in 1897.

AN ARTISTIC PLAY

At a time when the universal surge was towards naturalism (specifically, in France, Andre Antoine, *Theatre Libre* [Free Theater] and the legatees of [Emile] Zola), Rostand chose to aggrandize artifice and elevate whimsy. Even the nonnaturalistic esthetics of [Maurice] Maeterlinck [Belgian author] left him cold. His was a theatre of the heart pitted against the rigours of the mind eschewing the fashionable doctrine which revered the social sciences. He did not so much swim against the tide as straddle a branch above it and watch it flow in other directions. There is something gratifying about that kind of artistic aloofness in an age, like our own, when everyone else was metaphorically wearing pins and subscribing to one 'school' or another.

Immersing oneself in Rostand, I was constantly reminded of Thomas Rowe, the 18th century playwright who apart from being a hopeless Shakespeare-groupie was also one of his first editors and a successful playwright in his own right. Rowe was grossly derivative of Shakespeare and virtually nothing he wrote had the distinction or quality of his mentor, but he did produce a rapid, functional, eminently speakable kind of dramatic verse which made works such as *The Fair Penitent* and *Jane Shore* play with verve and efficacy. To discuss Rostand in the same breath as Molière or Corneille, Racine or Marivaux [French dramatists] is to relegate him to some lower echelon of creativity. But just as there are certain kinds of theatrical effects in which Rowe succeeds far better than Shakespeare, so there is a certain resilient romanticism in Rostand which one can find in almost no other French playwright—including Victor Hugo and [Alexandre] Dumas *fils* [Jr.] whose progeny he would appear to be. It is the sinuous and ebullient verse of a "minor" poet which, because of his sense of dramaturgy and intellectual independence, occasionally produces "major" effects.

STRAYING FROM THE NORM

The last thing Rostand is interested in is the well made play. He, like his rambunctious hero, instinctively recoils from anything as prefabricated as that. As A.G.H. Spier wrote in the twenties, Rostand's work "is divided into three parts which we might call the statement of the ideal, the test and the confirmation" and *Cyrano* clearly exemplifies this pattern. There are whole chunks of the play which, evaluated according to established playwriting techniques, could be deleted because they do not help the plot proceed to that point of resolution to which traditional plays usually tend. But if one did delete them, one would be losing the pearls that give the crown its glitter. Apply the traditional yardstick to a work like *The Importance of Being Earnest* [play by Oscar Wilde] and you could reach the same conclusion—but the virtues of that play, as with *Cyrano*, are in the amplifications, the digressions, the, if you like, irrelevancies. Sometimes it is texture which determines the quality of content and, in such cases, one must revere the peculiarities of a text as one does the peculiar characteristics of an individual who, outsize and unorthodox, is, for those very reasons, more fascinating.

ROMANTIC APPEAL

The play is predicated on the irresistible lie that wit, talent and personal panache cannot only compensate a man for physical ugliness but also enable him to triumph over competition which is patently more attractive. It is the pipe dream of every acne-ridden schoolboy and tubby, balding Romeo who watches the good-looking jock waltz off with the most desirable campus beauties. It elevates the idea of esthetic worth to a height as fanciful as it is unreal. Perhaps that is why the play is juvenile in the very best sense of that word and, for a century, has been so highly appreciated by very

young people. Its own intrinsic romanticism speaks persua-
sively to people who have not yet lost their sense of romance.
It is redolent of the fairy tales on which young persons have
been weaned. It is a literary extrapolation of "Beauty and the
Beast," "The Ugly Duckling" and all those other fables where
unprepossessing heroes improbably win the hands of fairy
princesses. In other words, it nourishes the fantasy quotient in
men and women which, unfortunately, attenuates as they
grow older and wiser—i.e. mundane and cynical. It is, if you
like, "children's theatre" on the very highest level—because,
mythic roots notwithstanding, its branches yield the ripe fruit
of culture and poetry. The hero of *Cyrano de Bergerac* is not
the eponymous hero based on the real adventurer and poet of
the mid 17th century but Poetry itself; the poetic notion of life
as opposed to its prosaic counterpart; fancy as opposed to fact;
dream-life as opposed to real-life. Cyrano's adventure, both in
the play and in his own life, exemplified the kind of action and
endeavor which is no longer available to us in our own lives—
except through emulation of make-believe heroes in books,
plays and films. That is why we continually come back to
Cyrano. He represents the freedom, independence, noncha-
lance and impetuosity which we barter away in order to become responsible citizens—qualities which we never forgive
the adult world from taking from us.

Cyrano, a National Hero

Hugh Allison Smith

Local color—a particular sense of the region and time portrayed—also plays a large role in *Cyrano de Bergerac*. Seventeenth-century France is often associated with romantic ideals that stress the importance of honor and wit. This sets the scene perfectly for a larger-than-life character such as Cyrano. In this excerpt from his book, *Main Currents of Modern French Drama*, Hugh Allison Smith discusses how Cyrano shines in this environment, an example of courage and sensitivity. Smith goes on to claim that this portrayal of Cyrano captures the essence of what it means to be French, making Cyrano a Gallic national hero. Hugh Allison Smith was a professor of romance languages at the University of Wisconsin. He has also written *A French Reader* and *The Composition of the* Chanson de Willame [Song of William].

Cyrano de Bergerac is the supreme dramatic achievement of Rostand. It is, moreover, the piece in which culminates the only distinct school of poetic drama that existed in France in the nineteenth century. It deserves, then, special consideration from both of these points of view.

It is, first of all, a Romantic drama. If it had appeared a half-century earlier, its evolution and place in dramatic development would have seemed easy to fix—at first sight. Coming as it does after a full generation of realistic literature, and with its author brought up in the Naturalistic atmosphere, it appears, in its brilliance and vigor, a strange phenomenon. Is it simply a flower of pure Romantic stock, blooming by some strange accident, in the wintry field of bleak realism after lying dormant for fifty years, or is it, af-

Excerpted from *Main Currents in Modern French Drama*, by Hugh Allison Smith (New York: Henry Holt, 1925).

ter all, a modified product of its species, showing the improvement of cultivation and the influence of the climate and soil in which it is grown?

The Romantic elements of *Cyrano* are unmistakable. In it Rostand conforms to practically all the theory of the Romanticists—but he also excels most of them in practice.

LOCAL COLOR

One of the important features of Romantic drama was local color—in historic drama this color should be the evocation of the spirit and atmosphere of the age represented. In this respect, the play is superior to any of the Romantic productions. With marvelous skill, the author makes live before us, in rapid, magic strokes, the turbulent audience that stood in the pit, the prankish page who fished up bourgeois wigs from the upper gallery, the foppish marquis who sat on the stage to show his court prerogatives and the ribbons and lace on his costume, and the *précieuses,* or romantic bluestockings [female intellectuals], such as Roxane and her friends, who peeped through their masks from the boxes. We are back in the seventeenth century, with its heroism and bombast, with its brave soldiers and bragging bullies, with its wigs and ruffs, with its clever women and witty men, its masks, its romance, its duels, with all the brave show of the most brilliant city, court and country of the epoch. And this color and history are not on the surface but come from the heart of the work. The plot of the play is made to depend on the preciosity, or super-refinement, of Roxane, and whether or not Rostand has brought to life the real historic Cyrano—a matter of absolutely no importance—he has placed him, as conceived, in the only atmosphere he could breathe and against a background that is both real and artistic. In doing this, he has much surpassed the usual Romantic practice. He does not choose some famous figure and deform it, as [Victor] Hugo and [Alexandre] Dumas often did, but he takes a comparatively obscure one and illuminates it, and at the same time lights up a whole page of interesting history.

MIXING GENRES

In its far-reaching effect, perhaps the most important innovation of the Romantic school was the mingling of the kinds: the combining of the sublime and the grotesque, or of the tragic and the comic, and the introduction of the lyrical element into drama. In these respects, *Cyrano* is truly a Romantic play. The comic side, and particularly its gaiety, wit and humor, are too obvious to call for specification. What is more interesting is that some of the best French critics have been inclined to see in this the chief merit and appeal of the play. However, this would be accepting a quality that is expressed in detail and on the surface as superior to one that is in the heart of the drama. It would be, moreover, equivalent to saying that *Cyrano*'s merit is purely transitory, good

A Helpless Cyrano

Seth Daniel Riemer, in National Biases in French and English Drama, *a book based on his doctoral thesis for Cornell University, presents another interpretation of Cyrano's sensitivity. Rather than a noble hero, he depicts Cyrano as a suffering artist whose self-defeating fears prevent him from acting on his desires.*

For all of his courage, imaginativeness, and bold spirits, Cyrano is both helpless and hapless. For him to assert his independence merely activates hidden, ominous forces already poised to bear down upon and crush him. Flailing about blindly in his rags to defend a scrap of gentility and grace, he strikes us as a ridiculous and lamentable clown. Indeed, the strain and sacrifice that he must endure on behalf of his ideals make them negative in thrust, self-defeating in aim.

Cyrano's intentions toward Roxane reveal in moving terms how surely the pursuit of those ideals—as well as the genius he demonstrates therein—must go awry. A yearning for acceptance, affirmation and connectedness underlies his feelings for her. Practically speaking, however, that yearning has stimulated a conviction of unworthiness, which, in turn, barred his approach toward her and so worked against his purpose. The longing to announce his passion openly was first daunted by an understandable fear of rejection; thus, to impress her and win her heart he had to conceal his true identity. By using the handsome (but brainless) Christian as his surrogate, he raised a factitious although insurmountable obstacle to the fulfillment of his desires. Though the strategy was clever, he gained only heartache from it and, in a sense, made matters worse for himself by creating a successful rival to his own affections.

Daniel Riemer, *National Biases in French and English Drama*, Garland Studies in Comparative Literature. NY: Garland, 1990.

for an evening's entertainment, and that it possesses no serious appeal that can be carried away and returned to, after the novelty is passed, with pleasure and profit.

CREATING A NATIONAL HERO

Cyrano is primarily a drama of elevated motives and this serious quality forms its lasting appeal. It is, above all, a play based on a single character and the chief motives of this character are honor, independence, and self-sacrifice, all factors of serious drama, and all most fundamental. On the first of these motives there is no need to insist. It is the key to Cyrano's character, as it is to that of most French dramatic heroes. It is the motive of his duels and other exploits, it is the sentiment that seals his lips on his love for Roxane, when Christian is killed, and it is his strength, in the end, to draw his sword against the approach of death in order to preserve his glory intact. It should be noted also that his is the traditional and national French honor: the *point d'honneur* [point of honor] of the Cid, feudal in its punctiliousness; the honor of Bayard, chivalric in its delicacy; and the honor of Roland, sublime, in its hopelessness.

CYRANO'S STRENGTH

Cyrano's independence is as strongly drawn as his honor, with which, moreover, it is closely united. Also, it is this quality which gives him his chief dramatic strength and differentiates him absolutely from the traditional Romantic hero, who is the pawn of fate and events, from a Hernani falling at the King's feet for pardon, or from a Ruy Blas changing his coat of prime minister for his valet's livery at the voice of his master. [Hernani and Ruy Blas are title characters from Hugo plays.] Never, perhaps, has this spirit of independence been more eloquently expressed than at the end of Cyrano's famous tirade against subserviency, where he states his own ideals:

> To sing, to laugh, to dream,
> To walk in my own way and be alone,
> Free, with an eye to see things as they are,
> A voice that means manhood—to cock my hat
> Where I choose—At a word, a *Yes*, a *No*,
> To fight—or write. To travel any road
> Under the sun, under the stars, nor doubt
> If fame or fortune lie beyond the bourne—
> Never to make a line I have not heard
> In my own heart; yet, with all modesty
> To say: "My soul, be satisfied with flowers,
> With fruit, with weeds even; but gather them

In the one garden you may call your own."
So, when I win some triumph, by some chance,
Render no share to Caesar— . . .

Act 2, scene 8

If this declaration were only the oratory of a Romantic hero, it would mean little, but we find that it is a code lived up to throughout the play.

Cyrano's self-sacrifice in his love for Roxane is no less a motive in the drama and furnishes occasion for most of the emotion of the play. He himself has stated perfectly this rôle in his death scene, when told that Molière had copied from him one of his greatest successes:

CYRANO
Yes—that has been my life. . . .
Do you remember that night Christian spoke
Under your window? It was always so!
While I stood in the darkness underneath,
Others climbed up to win the applause—the kiss!—
Well—that seems only justice—I still say,
Even now, on the threshold of my tomb—
"Molière has genius—Christian had good looks—"

Act 5, scene 6

This sacrifice and the idealization of an impossible love have already been referred to in *La Princesse Lointaine* [another play by Rostand]; it is a favorite theme with Rostand.

Like Hugo and other Romanticists, Rostand was a lyric poet and has introduced lyricism into his plays. There is, however, a notable difference when compared with Hugo. The latter constantly sought to create lyrical situations, often at the expense of his plot and character development. Rostand has maintained the lyrical element subordinate, and has used it only when it is in place and in order to add to the dramatic effect. . . .

EXPRESSING CYRANO'S SENSITIVITY

It is very largely the lyrical passages in *Cyrano* that should decide one of the most disputed questions in Rostand's poetry, his ability to evoke deep and sincere feeling, love or passion. No one denies him the gift to express graceful and agreeable sentiment and emotion, but it is often claimed that he does not have the deeper power. No doubt the highly etherealized and idealistic love that Rostand portrays by preference has contributed to form this opinion. Also, in *Cyrano* there is much intentional super-refinement. However, it is precisely in this play that Rostand has himself invited this test of his ability. In the well-known balcony scene, where Cyrano forgets Christian and speaks his own love to Roxane, the poet explicitly disavows, in sincere love, the elaboration of exquisite similes and highly alembicated sentiment. Here then, if anywhere, his words should express real feeling. The passage is too long to quote in its entirety, but the lines at the end are representative.

> —Oh, but to-night, now, I dare say these things—
> I . . . to you . . . and you hear them! . . . It is too much!
> In my most sweet unreasonable dreams,
> I have not hoped for this! Now let me die,
> Having lived. It is my voice, mine, my own,
> That makes you tremble there in the green gloom
> Above me—for you do tremble, as a blossom
> Among the leaves— You tremble, and I can feel,
> All the way down along these jasmine branches,
> Whether you will or no, the passion of you
> Trembling . . .

Act 3, scene 6

In the above passage, where the poet wishes to be most direct and simple, there are perhaps more elaboration and refinement of style than we are accustomed to associate with the expression of the deepest feeling. Certainly such style is far removed from the agonizing phrases of a victim of the heart in Dumas's *Dame aux Camélias*, or from the disconnected, passionate cries of a victim of the dramatist in [Victorien] Sardou's *Patrie*, but this may be none the less the natural language of a lyric poet. We should hardly expect him to make love in the language of the butcher or the baker, or even perhaps in the same style as that of the doctor or the banker. We can not apply here the criterions of realistic literature. Shakespeare certainly knew the true language of feeling, and moreover, possessing every key in the gamut of human expression, could strike the most realistic or even brutal note, when he wished, and yet the style of Shakespeare in an exactly similar scene has the same qualities. One has only to read three lines of Romeo's speech to be reminded of this fact:

> "It was the lark, the herald of the morn:
> No nightingale: look, Love, what envious streaks
> Do lace the severing clouds in yonder east:—"

THE ART OF DRAMA

The connection of Rostand's drama with Hugo's is too obvious to need comment, but there is one fundamental difference between these two authors: Rostand is a dramatist and Hugo is not. In demonstrating this fact from *Cyrano*, all the secondary factors of dramatic ability, those of detail or those which may be contained in a single scene, will be discarded. Hugo also could be effective within those limits, although it is doubtful if anything in Hugo can be found as perfect and sustained dramatically, without the false notes of melodrama, as the final act of *Cyrano*. In this last act, where Rostand has thrown the idealistic net of time, of nature and of religion over the stage, to soften before our eyes the more cruel lines of grief and terror in this tragedy of sacrifice and death, we have an almost perfect piece of sustained dramatic artistry. The quiet of the convent, the religious music and the autumn setting combine perfectly in a scene that is thoroughly dramatic and always appropriate. Such little touches as that of the falling leaves, symbolizing the imminent death of Cyrano, fit perfectly into a harmonious whole. . . .

THE IMPORTANCE OF CONSISTENT CHARACTERIZATION

But admittedly the more fundamental elements of drama are to be found in the creation of characters and their translation into action in a play, and, back of these, in the author's conception or philosophy of life, of which character and action are the products.

Hugo's characters are inconsistent, the products of antithesis, controlled by the arbitrary hand of the author, under the mask of blind fate, and his plots are as illogical as his dramatic figures. Cyrano is a consistent character, acting in every crisis in accordance with dominating motives, and coming to the end which we should expect the sum total of these qualities to produce. With his Quixotic honor, his keenly sensitive spirit of independence, which prevents his accepting the slightest favor or help, and with his exalted ideal of sacrifice, we anticipate his lack of worldly success, his death in poverty and his failure to win the woman he loves. Also, it is most important to note that in putting the real drama in the soul of Cyrano, developed by motives contained in this character, Rostand returns to the Classic practice initiated by Corneille of making drama interior, and creating dramatic heroes who are masters of their own fate.

There is, to be sure, antithesis in Cyrano's character—there is antithesis in the characters of *Hamlet* and of the *Misanthrope*—but it is not the author's basic conception. It is not *be-*

cause Cyrano is a poetic genius that he is a failure; it is not *because* he is made grotesque by a large nose that he is a tender and spiritual lover.

THE QUINTESSENTIAL FRENCH HERO

Whether in strict agreement with fact or not, Rostand has made him a poetic lover and a genuine hero, and has used his wit to keep sentiment from becoming sentimentality, and his sense of humor and irony to prevent Quixotic bravery from appearing as pure boasting and bravado. When Cyrano, moved by his hopeless love for Roxane, is about to weep, he is checked by the humorous thought of tears running down his big nose, and we are saved from the pit of pathos. When he stages his spectacular duel against the hundred men, he forestalls the charge of mock heroics by calling himself a "Scipio, triply nosed"; when in the end his independence and honor are exalted into hallucination and he draws his sword on the spectres of Cowardice, Stupidity and Death, he falls to the earth with a smile and a jest for his *panache.* And it is precisely this conception of the character of Cyrano that makes him most national and offers him the greatest promise of being immortal among French heroes.

Reckless bravery is a favorite quality in heroes of all times and countries, but there is something in Cyrano that is essentially French: his sense of the uselessness of the sacrifice and the light-heartedness with which it is made. As a symbol of these qualities, at least, his *panache* is truly and traditionally French and not simply Gascon; it is the plume of Henri IV [the first of the Bourbon kings of France] about which every Frenchman rallies.

The native good sense of the French is not duped by forlorn hopes, but their desire for the approval and admiration of their fellows, their social instinct, drives them to such exploits, and their irresistible racial gaiety enables them to jest in the face of death. Seek in French heroes of legend or literature at all times and you will find these same qualities of hopeless but light-hearted courage and Cyrano is one of the most recent of these national symbols.

Idealism in *Cyrano de Bergerac*

Charles Huntington Whitman

Critics have claimed that *Cyrano de Bergerac* lacks original characters and is, at best, an imitation of the great
writers. Dismissed as a failed attempt to revive romanticism—and as a mismatch of writing styles and techniques—it has also been criticized for its improbable situations. In this excerpt, Charles Huntington Whitman
asserts that the play has its faults, but that Rostand's idealism and the idealism demonstrated by his characters
infuse the play with undeniable charm. Whitman taught
at Rutgers University, edited books on poetry and
drama, and translated *The Christ of Cynewulf: A Poem
in Three Parts* into English prose.

Few writers have ever given themselves to art with such
whole-hearted devotion as did Rostand. A thorough-going
romanticist, he wrote to satisfy his own artistic conscience
rather than to win applause; indeed he never made the
slightest concession to the prevailing taste of the day. It was
as though the contemporary realistic drama did not exist for
him. As [novelist and journalist] Storm Jameson puts it:
"Modern drama ends for him with Victor Hugo, and he continues to embroider grand passions and high deeds with an
exuberant delight in color and rhythm. While Naturalism
gasps in the gutter and Realism wastes its last strength in
spasmodic energy, M. Rostand sings to himself in a forgotten
isle of romance, sings for the sheer joy of singing." It is little
wonder that the earlier plays of Rostand should have been so
eagerly welcomed by a public surfeited with the sordid and
sex-drenched plays of the day. To turn from such dramas to
Rostand with his chivalry, his lofty idealism, his zest for life,
is like the emerging from the gloom and tainted air of a sub-
way into pure atmosphere and bright sunlight.

Excerpted from *Representative Modern Dramas*, edited by Charles Huntington Whitman (New York: Macmillan, 1939). Copyright © 1936 by Charles Huntington Whitman.

A ROMANTIC REVIVAL?

The enthusiasm aroused by the appearance of Rostand's plays at first gave rise to the belief that France was about to experience a real revival of romanticism. The belief proved abortive, however, for as it turned out the genius of Rostand did not prove sufficiently robust to divert the strongly-running realistic stream into the channel of pure romance. [Jules] Lemaître's view that his plays are rather backward-looking than forward-looking, representing the distillation of French romanticism from [Pierre] Corneille down to [Jean] Richepin, has of late won rather general acceptance. In the opinion of this French critic *Cyrano de Bergerac* "prolongs, unites, and blends . . . three centuries of comic fantasy and moral grace." Thus Rostand was rather an isolated figure. He initiated no school of dramatists, and he exercised apparently but little influence either upon his contemporaries or upon his successors.

Rostand, like Victor Hugo, was a lyric poet, though he was far more successful than his distinguished predecessor in translating his lyricism into terms of the drama. His poetry is graceful and rich in color and verbal music, but its virtues are those of a brilliant virtuoso, not those of a major poet. Not infrequently its brilliancy seems metallic and artificial, its richness too dependent on excessive decoration and imagery. The critics of his own land in particular have been most severe upon him, looking with suspicion on his exuberance and romantic fervor. Even the admirers of Rostand cannot be blind to his obvious defects: his theatricalism, his emotionalism, the lack of originality in his plots, the superficiality of certain characters, especially on the distaff side. To his credit, however, may be cited virtues that go far to atone for any deficiencies: the eloquence and sparkling wit of many a purple passage, the elegance and refinement of style, and the pure idealism of his major characters. His plays offer a sure and delightful way of escape into the land of romance when the world is too much with us. . . .

THE PLAY'S POPULARITY

Cyrano de Bergerac, the most perennially popular of modern romantic plays, was produced in Paris, at the Théâtre de la Porte Saint-Martin, on the night of December 28, 1897, and attained an instantaneous success. A combination of favorable circumstances conspired to launch this child of fortune on its happy career. It happened to arrive at the very moment when the theatre-going public was becoming weary of the sordid realism of the Paris theatre, with its everlasting emphasis on sex; its hero was a dashing figure of romance, its author a poet of high reputation, its chief actor the recognized leader of the French stage. As for the play itself, it was, as one critic has phrased it: "a sort of artistic patchwork, using all the favorite French colors." Few plays, in fact, exhibit such a mingling of diverse elements—the sublime and the grotesque, the tragic and the comic, honor, bravery, romance, and sentiment—all fused into an harmonious whole through the magic of Rostand's pen. In it even the most jaded of theatre-goers is sure to find something to his taste. Its perennial popularity is "an index to the abiding tendency in humanity toward the romantic and the chivalrous." Among all the theories advanced to account for the peculiar appeal of the play perhaps the most acceptable is the oft-quoted statement of Madame Rostand: "Certain people exist who always inspire sympathy simply because they possess charm. Isn't it the same with the mind and what it creates?"

Cyrano de Bergerac cannot lay claim to any great originality. Its inspiration came not from life, but from literature. It is apparent that Rostand had learned certain lessons from the "well-made" plays of the French realists, particularly [Alfred de] Musset and [Pierre] Marivaux; it is evident too that he was influenced not a little by Shakespeare and Hugo, whose *Hernani* had been the reigning romantic play of its generation. In fact it is generally held that Rostand exemplifies the dramatic principles laid down by Hugo in the Preface to *Cromwell*, particularly the doctrine of the grotesque and the sublime, more completely than Hugo himself. The protagonist of *Cyrano de Bergerac* has its prototype in a Gascon soldier, philosopher, and man of letters of that name, noted for his boasting and his wit, who lived in the days of Molière. We have Rostand's own word for it that the figure of the historic Cyrano haunted him for years before he found the time ripe to put him in a play, which, once completed, recaptured with remarkable vividness the colorful and turbulent life of the seventeenth century. Yet, while he drew mainly upon historic sources, he drew also upon his own life-experiences for certain of the incidents in the career of the dramatic hero. The originality of the play, however, is to be found chiefly in the rich embroidery of the verse, and in the magnificent vitality with which the work is informed.

AN IDEAL HERO

Cyrano is a pure idealist, who ever asserts the supremacy of the spirit over the flesh. It is his idealism, his high sense of honor, his independence, his courage, the light-heartedness with which he struggles on in the face of almost certain failure, which make him a sympathetic and heroic figure in spite of his grotesqueness and his braggadocio. One does not think the less of him because of his boasting when one comes to realize that it is but a screen to cover up his extreme sensitivity. Once for an instant he lowers his guard and lays bare his very soul. The revelation comes in the scene at the *Hôtel de Bourgogne* when his friend Le Bret is urging him to declare his love to Roxane. "What? Through my nose? [Cyrano interposes.] She might laugh at me. That is the one thing in this world I fear."

[Author and critic] Clayton Hamilton declares that Cyrano is guilty of the crime of self-sacrifice, saying: "I call self-sacrifice a crime, for . . . the primary object of life is not self-sacrifice but self-fulfillment." The question raised admits of no final answer. May it not be, however, that Cyrano best fulfilled himself through renunciation and through keeping his white plume unsullied? Cyrano, according to his own confession, wishes to be admirable (*"J'ai décidé d'être admirable, en tout, pour tout!"* [I have decided to make myself in all things admirable]—Act I. Sc. 5), but he is eager also to be admired. There is a strong histrionic strain in his character, and his bravado is due in part to his desire to make a big impression (*"Mais quel geste!"* [But what a gesture!]—Act I. Sc. 4). It is significant that the last foe he fights in the closing scene is "vanity," which [English poet] Milton called: "That last infirmity of noble mind."

STRENGTHS AND FLAWS

Cyrano de Bergerac is termed an "heroic comedy," and rightly so—filled as it is with the gusto of life, with scenes of pure comedy. The core of the drama, however, lies in the tortured soul of Cyrano. The most insistent note is that of pathos rather than of tragedy. There is of course tragedy in the inability of Cyrano, while conscious of his great powers, to appear before the world as he really is, in his failure to realize his heart's desire, but (to quote Edward Everett Hale,

Jr.) he "carries it all off with a vitality that makes us almost forget the tragedy."

It is easy to find defects in the play. The scenes, while individually interesting and effective, are by no means fused into a perfect unity. In fact, the play owes what unity it possesses chiefly to the persistence of the hero, who dominates the action as completely as does Hamlet in Shakespeare's masterpiece. There are, moreover, certain manifest improbabilities: the skill displayed by Cyrano in composing an intricate ballade during the duel, the sudden appearance of Roxane in the besieged camp of the Gascons, the prolongation of the final death scene. But these seem to fade into insignificance before the positive merits of this play, so rich in its poetry, so inspiring in its idealism.

CHAPTER 3

The Trouble with Translation

Staging and Adapting
Cyrano de Bergerac

Anthony Burgess

A writer creates a play with the hope that it will be
staged and performed. When a play remains popular
as long as *Cyrano de Bergerac* has, it is sometimes
adapted so that modern audiences will understand
and appreciate the subtleties and references. In
Cyrano de Bergerac's case, issues of translation also
come into play. A word-for-word translation that
keeps its artistic value is impossible for something
originally written in rhyming verse. In this introduction to his second translation of *Cyrano de Bergerac,*
Anthony Burgess addresses how he dealt with these
issues. Burgess has been a Distinguished Professor
at the City College of New York and his works include *A Clockwork Orange, The End of the World
News: An Entertainment, The Kingdom of the Wicked,
The Enderby Trilogy,* and *Ninety-Nine Novels: The
Best in English Since 1939.*

This rendering of Rostand's *comédie héroïque en cinq actes
en vers* [heroic comedy in five acts in verse] was commissioned for production by the Royal Shakespeare Company at
the Barbican Theatre in London in the summer of 1983. But
I had previously been commissioned, thirteen years earlier
in fact, to translate and adapt the work for the Tyrone
Guthrie Theater in Minneapolis, Minnesota, USA. It was
proposed that Christopher Plummer play the lead, but the
part was taken instead by Paul Hecht. That was in the summer of 1971. The following year a Broadway musical was
made out of this version, with lyrics by myself and music by
the Welsh film composer Michael Lewis. In this Plummer
played the lead—his first and last singing role (I do not think
his few *parlando* interjections in *The Sound of Music* can be

termed singing). The musical opened at a bad time—the time of the Watergate revelations—and it suffered from union problems. Moreover, though I participated in what amounted to a vulgarization of the original—chiefly in the hope of making money which I did not, in fact, make—I had always had my doubts about the musicalization of *Cyrano de Bergerac*, as it had seemed to me that there was already enough music in the words. I worked too hard on the editing, fresh adaptation and provision of new lyrics (a total of eighty-one, I remember). Perpetually changing *Cyrano*, as the musical was called, to make it more acceptable to a fairly indifferent public, was a daily business, and it was like working on the repair of an aircraft in flight. I was at the time doing a full-time academic job as Distinguished Professor at the City College of New York; I was also helping aspiring writers in a creative writing course; I was also lecturing all over the United States at various universities. It was too much.

SATISFYING A MODERN AUDIENCE

The Tyrone Guthrie Theater version (published by Knopf in December 1971 and still in print) was commissioned by the artistic director of the theatre, Michael Langham, and he proposed that the original text be somewhat radically changed. Of all the characters in the play, the least satisfactory to a modern audience appeared to be Roxane (whose name was degallicized to Roxana). She loves Christian, and yet she rebuffs him because he cannot woo her in witty and poetic language. This must seem very improbable in an age that finds a virtue in sincere inarticulacy, and I was told to find an excuse for this near-pathological dismissal of a good wordless soldier whose beauty, on her own admission, fills Roxane's heart with ravishment. So I inserted a little speech which I hoped would ring plausibly, to the effect that inarticulate brutish wooing was a mark of the aristocracy that would regard a middle-class bookish pretty girl like Roxane as fair game, and that to her the advent of true love must reveal itself in divine eloquence. This was meant to add a human substratum to Roxane's preciosity. On the American stage it seemed to work.

But, adding to her lines in Act III, I had to subtract her entire physical presence from Act IV. Her sudden appearance outside the walls of besieged Arras, with gifts of wine, cold

chicken and sausage for the starving Gascony cadets, relieved the tension of a scene which, the director insisted,
should remain taut to the end, and it was felt that it relieved
it in an unworthy manner—through farce and the atmosphere of a fairy tale. Apart from the difficulty of staging (and
it is this scene more than anything which puts good amateur
companies off the play), everything that is good in this phase
of the action seemed to the director to go bad as soon as Roxane came on in her coach and Paris perfume. The hungry
cadets cease to be heroic and become merely foppish. They
are nearly dying of starvation, and yet they have to go
through the motions of taking an elegant little dinner, complete with cutlery and napery. They become mean; they
make sure that de Guiche, their detested colonel, who is as
ill from hunger as they are, gets nothing of their feast. We
may be persuaded, with difficulty, that they now feel fine,
but there is a nasty taste in our mouths. Then comes Roxane's avowal to Christian: it is his soul she loves, she tells
him, not his physical beauty: she would prefer him to be
ugly so that his spiritual qualities may shine the more. All
this is on a battlefield, with death ready to arrive at any moment. The whole thing, so Michael Langham believed, became absurd, farcical, unacceptable in terms of even the
most far-fetched dramatic convention. He said it had to go,
so it went.

I had to substitute for Roxane's personal appearance the
arrival of a letter from her, which she, distant and disem-
bodied, had to breathe into a microphone while the lights
dimmed and perfume was sprayed through the auditorium.
I was amused to find Langham's radical desire for such a
change abetted by a Mr. Magoo cartoon film, in which Mr.
Magoo, playing Cyrano, returns amid shells and snipers
from mailing the daily letter to Roxane with a letter from the
beloved herself in his hand. Roxane's Platonic rhetoric
comes off well enough when we can take it as epistolary literature, but, to some, and certainly to Langham, it sounds
unreal on speaking lips.

THE ADAPTER'S PREROGATIVE

I made, on my own initiative, a less fundamental change in
Act III. Roxane and Christian are being hurriedly married by
a Capuchin duped into performing the act, and Cyrano has
to prevent de Guiche—who wants Roxane as a mistress and

has, through his uncle Cardinal Richelieu, power over the entire Capuchin order—from discovering that the ceremony is taking place and stopping it. In the original, Cyrano pretends to have fallen from outer space and he insists on telling de Guiche—who does not see the outsize nose and thinks he is being accosted by a madman—the various possible ways of getting to the moon. Since, at the time of the first production of my version, we had not long been celebrating the moon landing, it seemed that there was a danger that the audience might feel very superior to Cyrano (who, incidentally, as a historical personage wrote the world's first science fiction) and ignore his ingenuity while wanting to put him right on rocketry. So I wrote a couple of speeches in the satirical vein of the historical Cyrano, which could be taken as prefiguring the polemic indiscretion that (in the play, fifteen years later) is the cause of his assassination. It does not greatly matter what Cyrano does to prevent de Guiche's discovery of the clandestine wedding, since it is merely a matter of filling in time entertainingly. Damn it, he could dance and sing, as Christopher Plummer eventually did.

Michael Langham suggested merging the characters of Le Bret and Carbon de Castel-Jaloux to make one meaty personage instead of two thin ones. I did this. I also, at his behest, had the poet Lignière recite some lines from the libellous poem that is the cause of Cyrano's fight with a hundred armed ruffians. It was my own idea to make Cyrano improvise a kind of acrostic on his name in Act II, instead of leaving it to a poet to go home and do it for him. For the rest, the Tyrone Guthrie Theater version was close enough to the play as Rostand wrote it, except for one or two lops of Occam's razor.

STAYING CLOSE TO THE ORIGINAL

The [1984] version . . . has many passages in common with that American Ur-adaptation (those two additions just mentioned, for instance), but it represents an almost total return to Rostand's text. A translator-adaptor is a servant of the originating producer or director. Formerly a servant of Michael Langham and of Michael Kidd (for the Broadway musical version), I became a servant of Terry Hands, the director of the Royal Shakespeare Company. He, a French scholar, did not want too many departures from Rostand. He also wanted an English version which should be in neither

THE MEANING OF *PANACHE*

The last word—and some say the spirit as well—of Cyrano de Bergerac *is* panache. *Because Edmond Rostand partly added new meaning to the word, some translators substitute "plume" for panache, a very literal meaning.*

[When] Rostand took his seat at the Académie française, in his traditional discours de réception [reception speech], he proposed to his fellow academicians a definition of panache:

> To joke in the face of danger is the supreme politeness, a delicate refusal to cast oneself as a tragic hero; panache is therefore a timid heroism, like the smile with which one excuses one's superiority. Heroes lacking panache are certainly more disinterested than others, since, in making a sacrifice panache often brings with it an attitude of consolation. A little frivolous perhaps, most certainly a little theatrical, panache is nothing but a grace but a grace which is so difficult to retain in the face of death, a grace which demands so much strength that, all the same, it is a grace . . . which I wish for all of us.

Nicholas Cronk, Introduction to *Cyrano de Bergerac*, Christopher Fry, trans. New York: Oxford University Press, 1996.

prose, blank verse nor relentless heroic couplets. In other words, something on the lines of the Tyrone Guthrie Theater version, but without too many fanciful reworkings of the original.

THE DIFFICULTIES OF TRANSLATION

The original American commission was the result of long dissatisfaction with the version of *Cyrano de Bergerac* that Brian Hooker made for Walter Hampden and published in 1923, and which—with many directorial cuts—Michael Langham had used for a production at Stratford, Ontario, in 1963, when Christopher Plummer played the lead for the first time.

The Hooker translation (often termed facetiously the unhappy Hooker) is still the standard version used in America, though my own is beginning to supersede it, and it was the basis for the film of the play in which José Ferrer starred. It achieved a kind of literary sanctity as the Random House Modern Library of the World's Best Books definitive and undislodgeable Everybody's Cyrano, and this status is not undeserved. Hooker was a respectable minor poet, and, like many minor poets of the twenties, very skilful with tradi-

tional minor poetic forms like the ballade and the triolet—
both represented in *Cyrano*—as well as possessing a knack
with blank verse. Moreover, he had the humility to stick very
close to Rostand, and he does not cut one line: his translation can very nearly be used as a key to the original. But he
was not so slavish as not to recognize that certain literary
references in Rostand would not easily be caught by non-
French audiences. Thus, in Cyrano's long speech about his
nose, he substitutes 'Was this the nose that launched a thousand ships?' for

> Enfin, parodiant Pyrame en un sanglot:
> 'Le voilà donc ce nez qui des traits de son maître
> A détruit l'harmonie! Il en rougit, le traître!'

Here Rostand is referring to a tragedy [17th-century drama
Pyrame et Thisbé] known to a Paris audience but not to any
likely to fill a theatre in London, New York or Minneapolis.
Encouraged by Hooker's ingenuity, but unhappy about his
failure to render the poignant tone of the original, I tried the
following equivalent of the Pyrame parody:

> And finally, with tragic cries and sighs,
> The language finely wrought and deeply felt:
> 'Oh that this too too solid nose would melt!'

But, if I had not read Hooker, I might have translated Rostand's lines more or less literally, thus losing a climax and a
comic-heroic effect.

PRODUCING A COMEDY

Hooker's translation, then, is both faithful and bold, but it
never works on the stage, or on the late-late television
screen, with the zing and bite or (since we have to use the
word sooner or later when discussing Cyrano or *Cyrano*)
panache we have a right to expect. Hooker has produced a
play in *cinq actes* and *vers*, but he has not produced a
comédie héroïque. Rostand is funny, as well as pathetic and
sentimental, but Hooker rarely raises a laugh. For that matter, his pathos is sometimes too mawkish for comfort, and
when we are moved it is very frequently in spite of the
words. The trouble lies, I think, in Hooker's decision to use
blank verse, a medium that ceased to be dramatically viable
about 1630. Overwhelmingly rich in Shakespeare, solid,
chunky, sometimes magnificent in Ben Jonson, packed and
astringent in [Philip] Massinger, blank verse became, in the
nineteenth-century revivalist tradition that Hooker followed,

an over-limpid or limping medium full of self-conscious Shakespearian echoes and somewhat remote—which the blank verse of the Elizabethans and, even more so, Jacobeans was not—from the rhythms of ordinary speech. Hooker makes Cyrano sound like a man speaking blank verse:

> What would you have me do?
> Seek for the patronage of some great man,
> And like a creeping vine on a tall tree
> Crawl upward, where I cannot stand alone?
> No, thank you! Dedicate, as others do,
> Poems to pawnbrokers? Be a buffoon
> In the vile hope of teasing out a smile
> On some cold face?

Elizabethan characters, on the other hand, sound like men imposing their own idiolects on a fundamental beat of iambic pentameters that is, so to speak, the unconscious and disregarded pulse of the play.

TRANSLATION ISSUES

Rostand, of course, wrote in rhymed alexandrines, like the great classical French dramatists, tragic and comic alike, and this metric ought strictly to be rendered into English heroic couplets:

> What would you have me do?
> Seek out a powerful protector, pursue
> A potent patron? Cling like a leeching vine
> To a tree? *Crawl* my way up? Fawn, whine
> For all that sticky candy called success?
> No, thank you. Be a sycophant and dress
> In sickly rhymes a prayer to a moneylender?
> Play the buffoon, desperate to engender
> A smirk on a refrigerated jowl?

Not, certainly, the very regular couplets of Pope, which no living writer can easily imitate, but five-beat lines with a varying number of syllables and a regular couplet rhyming scheme. Sprung or counterpoint rhythm, to use Gerard Manley Hopkins's terms, not strict decasyllables. I read and saw performed Richard Wilbur's translation of Molière's *Tartuffe,* in which he clings doggedly to rhymed decasyllabic couplets, and, in my first draft of *Cyrano* in translation, I tried to follow his example. Christopher Fry's version for the Chichester Theatre is in strict couplets, and I do not think it works any more than my first effort did. French alexandrines can be used in many ways, and the classical comic way, which is Molière's, is conventional, unpoetic, arhetorical: the metric seems to symbolize the social order and it is not available for the special expressive purposes of any individual character. Rostand is a late Romantic, and his alexandrine, though sometimes merely traditional and conventional (the tuning-up violins in Act I have to accommodate their *la* to it), becomes sometimes a highly rhetorical medium as well as a clever instrument of stichomythia. The English heroic couplet, with its mostly intellectual associations, cannot do as much. And the double clop of rhyme, always expected, always fulfilled, though admirable for moral or philosophical discourse, is difficult to sustain in a play which contains a lot of action and sudden surprises.

TO RHYME OR NOT?

My final decision was to use *some* rhyme, but to avoid couplets except for Cyrano's big scenes, which have an insolence or lyrical self-confidence to which the relentless unvarying clang of couplets seemed appropriate. Very frequently, the auditor will register rhyme irregularly placed, and for that matter verse rhythm itself, only subliminally. Rhyme is deliberately muffled at times, but there are occasions when it has to assert itself and snap out wittily. Take, for example, the passage in which de Guiche tells Cyrano that, Quixote-like, he is fighting windmills and that it may happen that

> Un moulinet de leurs grands bras chargé de toiles
> Vous lance dans la boue!

To which Cyrano replies: 'Ou bien dans les étoiles!' [or perhaps to the stars!] That is not, by English standards, a true rhyme, but to French ears it is witty, exact and subtly punning. In Hooker's version, de Guiche says that the windmills

> May swing round their huge arms and cast you down
> Into the mire.

And Cyrano answers: 'Or up—among the stars!' This is romantic enough, the tone of a diluted Mercurio, but Cyrano is being neat as well as bold. He needs the wit of rhyme. My version goes:

> De Guiche. If you fight with windmills, they'll swing
> their heavy spars
> And spin you down to the mud.
>
> CYRANO.   Or up to the stars.

As Hopkins said of his *Eurydice*, the reader, if he reads the kind of verse I have contrived here with his eyes, and not his ears, will get a brutal impression of 'raw nakedness'. The needs of speaking actors have come before the desire for prosodic neatness. Though I sustain a basic five-beat rhythm throughout the greater part of the translation, this is sometimes deliberately allowed to collapse: in the final act the line often breaks down totally, leaving a gasping kind of *vers libre* [free verse]. The true test of the verse technique, such as it is, rests in stage performance. This is not a poem but a play.

Verse or Prose?

Louis Untermeyer

The first translation is rarely the last. Each new translation brings with it new meaning to the work. The work itself might even translate form—moving from a play to a musical, opera, or movie. Depending on the intended audience, a single "best" translation might not exist. In this excerpt, Louis Untermeyer gives the motivation for his translation of *Cyrano de Bergerac*. He also provides an overview of various early translations. Louis Untermeyer was an American anthologist and poet, well-known for his literary collections. His works include *Modern American Poetry, The World's Great Stories,* and *Long Feud.*

The first performance of *Cyrano de Bergerac* was literally an historic occasion. The premiere, December 28, 1897, had been awaited with public curiosity and private apprehension. On the opening night Rostand was overcome with nervousness and overwhelmed with surprise. A half-hour before the curtain rose he apologized to the company for having involved them in what was sure to be a disastrous failure; two hours after the curtain had been rung down, the audience was still in the theatre, still applauding, still calling for the author, still crying out names and repeating lines in unprecedented excitement. The great French actor, Constant Coquelin, to whom the play was dedicated and who created the title-role, gives a picture of the scene:

> The first night was eagerly awaited by the critics, the literary, and the artistic worlds. The audience that night was undoubtedly the cream of our Parisian public. When the curtain rose on the first act there was not a seat vacant in the theatre. The emotion of a great event was floating in the air. Never, never have I lived through such a night. Victor Hugo's greatest triumph, the first night of *Hernani,* was the only theatrical event that can compare with it, and that was injured by the enmity of a clique who persistently hissed through the performance. There is but one phrase to express the enthusiasm at

our first performance—'a house in delirium' alone gives any idea of what took place. As the curtains fell on each succeeding act the entire audience would rise to its feet, shouting and cheering for ten minutes at a time. The coulisse and the dressing-rooms were packed by the critics and the author's friends, beside themselves with delight. I was trembling so that I could hardly get from one costume into another, and had to refuse my door to every one. Amid all this confusion Rostand alone seemed unconscious of his victory.

TRANSLATIONS AROUND THE WORLD

Thereafter, *Cyrano* became a permanent part of the international theatre. It was translated into every European language and several Oriental tongues, including Japanese. In the excellent German version by the eminent author, Ludwig Fulda, the play was performed again and again.

Its peculiar combination of classic manner and baroque style, of beauty and bombast, was a challenge to all translators. There have been at least half a dozen notable English versions. Within a year of its first French presentation four English texts were published: a readable if not too accurate version by two Englishwomen, Gladys Thomas and Mary F. Guillemard; a fairly idiomatic version by Gertrude Hall; a discreet prose rendering by Helen B. Dole, who felt that the ballade and other "arias" were untranslatable and printed them in French, "in their native melody and rhythm"; and a workmanlike approximation by Howard Thayer Kingsbury. It was Kingsbury's version that was presented to a New York audience on October 3, 1898 (less than a year after the Paris opening) with Richard Mansfield in the title role and Margaret Anglin playing the part of Roxane. On the same night another version of Rostand's drama was produced in Philadelphia by Augustin Daly with Charles Richman as Cyrano and Ada Rehan as Roxane.

THE PLAY'S EVOLUTION

The play continued to be so successful that it was almost immediately retailored. It became a comic opera which opened in New York on September 18, 1899. "Based" on Edmond Rostand's play, it had a book by Stuart Reed, lyrics by Harry B. Smith, and music by Victor Herbert. The title role was played by the favorite comic of the day, Francis Wilson.

On November 1, 1923, a new English version of what, by that time, was known as "the Rostand classic" featured Walter Hampden in a spirited verse adaptation by Brian Hooker.

An operatic arrangement with music by Walter Damrosch was staged in 1930. The text was by the music critic, W. J. Henderson, but the opera failed to win a place either in critical esteem or in the music-lover's heart.

The Hooker version was revived on October 8, 1946, with incidental music by the novelist-musician, Paul Bowles. The revival was staged by José Ferrer, who also acted the title part. Four years later Ferrer appeared in a brilliantly conceived film version, retaining a great part of the original play in Hooker's adaptation.

Two recent versions attempted to capture the swift-running rhymes of the original. The first, highly stylized and desperately spirited, was by the late English poet, Humbert Wolfe. This rendering was made for a film version that was to be produced in England starring Charles Laughton, but was abandoned. The other and more literal rhymed translation was published in Los Angeles in 1947. This was a collaboration, the joint product of Clifford Hershey Bissell, Ph.D., and William Van Wyck, Litt. D., a serious if not always successful effort.

It is a platitude to say that the transferring of a poetic work from one language to another involves many difficulties and results in many losses, but that platitude must be repeated. The fusing of separate phrases and stray ideas into a new thing complete in itself—the magic metamorphosis which is poetry—is untranslatable. The translator can expect nothing more than a fair approximation, a paraphrase, which will not sacrifice too much of the meaning at the expense of the music or, contrariwise, give up too much of the music to preserve the meaning. All he can hope for is a good compromise which will keep the rhythm pulsing, the action moving, and the spirit soaring.

THE EFFECTS OF RHYME

The question of rhyme demands separate consideration. In a play of any length, and particularly in a serious play, rhyme is a hazard. This is not true in France, where identities of sound, assonances, and echoes are used freely; in Rostand's language rhyme presents no problems to the Gallic ear. But the English actor—as well as the English audience—is accustomed either to a dramatic prose or variations of the resonant, rolling, and generally unrhymed blank verse perfected by the great Elizabethans. It is this variably sonorous but never cloying speech which has been maintained from the time of Marlowe and Shakespeare to T.S. Eliot and Christopher Fry. On our stage, and especially the modern stage, a long play in rhymed verse sounds both artful and artificial. Worse, it is difficult to follow. The listener grows intent upon the technical device; he waits for the rhymed word which is to cap its predecessor at the end of every line. In his attention to the sound he loses the sense.

TRANSLATOR'S MOTIVATION

Thus, in a completely rhymed translation of *Cyrano*, the too nimble pairing of sounds, the continual matching of similar syllables, the very insistence of the rhymes, is a danger which is also a disservice to the original. For, despite the label, *Cyrano* is a comedy only in a very special sense. It certainly is not a comic comedy—there are countless witticisms, plays on words, puns, and occasional grotesque episodes; but there is nothing essentially humorous in the action. The plight of an ugly man in love with a beautiful woman, an intellectual who woos his beloved for a stupid but handsome man, and loses her himself—this is the substance of a partly ironic, partly pathetic, and finally tragic drama. This is precisely the kind of play which Rostand wrote. The mood throughout is romantic; the language is rich; the tone is alternately sentimental and noble. In short, if it is a comedy at all, it justifies the subtitle which Rostand gave his play: A Comedy-Heroic.

The subtitle is the core of the drama. For "Cyrano" is heroic in the literal as well as the theatrical sense. Here, on one level, is a swashbuckler whose life is a perpetual physical and verbal challenge; a purple patchwork of dazzling swordplay accompanied by the most extravagant rhetoric. And here, on another level, is a man doomed by his own arrogant brilliance. What seems to be romanticism run riot is checked by a grim and even devastating irony. Cyrano's defiant posturing, his grandiose gestures and oratorical fanfares, turn out to be fragments of a career in ruins—a half-braggart, half-hopeless structure of defense, a triumph of despair. Like that other anachronistic grotesque, Don Quixote, Cyrano can face himself only in the cracked mirror of illusion.

THE USE OF VERSE

In an atmosphere of such contradictory luxuriance, the present translator has attempted to steer a middle course be-

tween the Scylla of plain prose and the Charybdis of highly
colored couplets. He recognizes that Rostand used a language which is so flexible, so melodious and delicately ar-
chaic, that even the most opulent prose fails to suggest the
musical character of the work. Therefore, since poetry in
one language can be suggested only by poetry in another,
blank verse has been chosen as the logical medium—a
blank verse which is chiefly colloquial rather than classical,
avoiding inversions, straightforward in idiom and modern in
tone. However, the famous duelling ballade and other set
pieces call for a much more formal treatment. Such lyrical
moments are so surcharged with high spirits and exuberance that they inevitably rise, or erupt, into rhyme. Here, as
in the body of the blank verse, the translator has tried to
strike a balance between the literal meaning of the original
text and Rostand's wit, fluency, and flickering eloquence.

   Cyrano de Bergerac is little more than half a century old—
not a long time in the life of a classic. It continues to be so
great a challenge to the interpreter that, within fifty years,
no less than ten English translators have offered their ren-
derings, each one vying with his predecessor in a fresh effort to bring the spirit of the original to the printed page. This
version is one more evidence of the play's continuing appeal.
Next to writing his own poetry, there is no greater pleasure
for a poet than putting into his own tongue the essence of
another poet. It is a dangerous delight, and the present para-
phraser hopes he has not too much adulterated Rostand's
sparkling words and potent music.

Translating the Play

Clayton Hamilton

Any given work can have a number of translations. To choose the best one, it helps to understand the motivation and techniques employed in the translation. For example, the purpose of a translation might be to reach a broader audience, address those who do not know the original language, or to surpass previous unsatisfactory translations. With these factors in mind, a translator has a great responsibility to also correctly and skillfully communicate the original's meaning and intent. In this introduction to Brian Hooker's translation of *Cyrano de Bergerac*, Clayton Hamilton reveals the motivation and generation of this well-known version. Clayton Hamilton is the author of such works as *A Manual of the Art of Fiction, Materials and Methods of Fiction,* and *Friend Indeed: A Comedy-Drama in Three Acts.*

Many years ago the late Augustin Daly made a brief revival in New York of *Love's Labor's Lost,* the earliest and in most respects the poorest of the plays of Shakespeare. There had been no public demand for the piece; there was no popular approval of the presentation: but, when a friend asked Mr. Daly why he had spent his money in such an undertaking, the manager replied, "My brother, the judge, had never seen the play and asked me for an opportunity to have a look at it."

REVIVING *CYRANO*

I had this anecdote in mind when, after enduring two decades of unremitted theatre-going made dreary by the absence from our stage of the most intoxicating play of modern times, I asked Walter Hampden to let me have another look at *Cyrano de Bergerac.* This request called for the raising of many thousands of dollars, the renting of a theatre in New York, the selection and long training of a company educated

Excerpted from the Preface, by Clayton Hamilton, to *Cyrano de Bergerac,* by Edmond Rostand, translated by Brian Hooker (New York: Henry Holt, 1923).

to speak verse and skilled in the rendition of romantic drama, the preparation of an elaborate production, and the study and composition of one of the most exacting parts in the entire history of the stage; but I had an altruistic argument to support an appeal that had been, in the first place, merely personal. *"Cyrano,"* I said, "has not been shown in New York for nearly a quarter of a century, except at one or two negligible matinées. This means, though it is hard for us to realize the fact, that all our theatre-goers under thirty years of age have been robbed of an experience that we ourselves remember as one of the most tingling of our 'teens. I want to see *Cyrano* again; but I am thinking also of the thousands of younger people who have never seen it at all. Won't you give them a chance?"

Not wishing me to carry my grey hairs in sorrow to an early grave, Mr. Hampden generously said, "I'll do the play for you if you will find me a translation. I have never read one." "Neither have I," I answered; for both of us had been bilingual since boyhood and our enthusiasm for Rostand had been derived entirely from our early habit of chanting his bravura passages in the French original. But if Mr. Hampden was not to be daunted by the difficulties of production, I was not to be put off by the problem of an English text. "Study the part in French," I said, "and ask Claude Bragdon to design the scenery. Meanwhile, I'll get you a translation."

IN SEARCH OF A GOOD TRANSLATION

After a visit to a bookstore, I read, for the first time in my life, half a dozen translations into English of *Cyrano de Bergerac*; and I hope that I shall never again experience so miserable a sense of disillusionment. One or two of them were so bad that they were not worth the paper they had been printed on. Two were more than tolerable; but, though fairly faithful to the letter of the French original, they seemed to me to miss entirely its spirit. The zest, the fire, the spontaneity, the brilliancy, the lyric rapture of Rostand were lacking. I felt as annoyed as a musician condemned to listen to the murder of a composition of Mozart's by a child at the piano, continually striking sharp or flat; and, by no effort of my inward ear, could I imagine Mr. Hampden, accustomed as he was to the lines of *Hamlet* and *Othello,* speaking such pedestrian and uninspired English in a poetic part that had been written by Rostand for the incomparable voice of Coquelin.

But if Walter Hampden was willing to let me have a look at the play, it seemed only fair for me to ask another of my friends to make a translation which Mr. Hampden should be able to speak and I should be able to read. I went to Brian Hooker. I asked him abruptly if he had ever read a translation of *Cyrano de Bergerac;* and, on receiving the expected negative response, I assured him that his estate was the more gracious. I then informed him that it was his duty to drop whatever he was doing, retire to the country for a couple of months, and translate *Cyrano* for Walter Hampden. Thus, in this practical age, are poets pestered by their friends.

Since that is the way in which this new version of *Cyrano de Bergerac* happened to be undertaken, the translator and the actor-manager have asked me to introduce the text to the reading public with a prefatory gesture. I am happy, indeed, to do so; for whatever may be the fate of the revival with the theatre-going public [this preface being written necessarily in advance of the event] I know already that Brian Hooker has succeeded in a literary task of extraordinary difficulty, that he has written a text which is both speakable and readable, and that he has made the vivid spirit of Edmond Rostand accessible, for the first time in a quarter of a century, to English-reading lovers of *belles-lettres* who are not able to read French.

HOOKER'S NEW VERSION

Mr. Hooker has asked me to explain the principles he had in mind in undertaking this new version. In the first place, since he was making it directly for production on the stage and only incidentally for publication, he wrote it by the ear and for the ear. While preserving the metres and the rhyme-schemes of the incidental lyrics, he chose blank verse as the medium for the dialogue, because, of course, the Alexandrine couplet would have sounded too outlandish to our theatre-going public. His verse is brisk, succinct, and crystal clear: it is easy for the actors to speak, and it is easy for the audience to understand without a moment's hesitation. It was far from Mr. Hooker's purpose to write a literal translation—the sort of rendering which, plodding faithfully from word to word, might be used as a "trot" by high-school students cramming for an examination in the French original. Not a line has been omitted from Rostand's text and not a line has been added to it. It is not to be thought for a moment that either Mr. Hooker or Mr. Hampden would have presumed to alter the play in any detail even though such sacrilege has often been committed under the *camouflage* of "adaptation"; but, in rendering many lines and speeches, the American poet has paraphrased the French original, instead of translating it *verbatim.* He has allowed himself this liberty in order to convey more clearly to Mr. Hampden's audience the theatrical thrust or the poetical point intended by Rostand. For instance, in the Ballade of the Duel, there is a line which reads, in the original, *"Elégant comme Céladon"* [Elegant like Céladon]; but, knowing that nobody in an American audience could be expected to have heard of Céladon, Mr. Hooker has substituted an illusion to Sir Launcelot, a hero whom Cyrano himself might have mentioned just as naturally as a symbol of the chivalrous and courtly. Only to pedants who know nothing of the necessities of the theatre will such a process seem unscholarly; but there may be, in our universities, a few undramatic critics for whom it will be necessary to explain that Mr. Hampden, while fighting a duel and improvising a ballade, cannot pause to step down to the footlights and issue a literary footnote to the audience. And those members of the American audience who are scholarly enough to recognize, in Cyrano's bravura speech about his nose, a delightful phrase from Marlowe's *Dr. Faustus,* will know that this has been substituted for a French quotation which was equally familiar to the Parisian audience. On the one hand, it is not unlikely that the actual Cyrano, who was both a playwright and a scholar, was familiar with Marlowe's address to Helen; and, on the other hand, the American auditor would have received no kick from a literal translation of the French quotation used in the original.

To sum the matter up, Mr. Hooker was commissioned, not to write a textbook or a "trot," but to write a play and a poem. His thought, like that of Rostand before him, was always of the theatre, always of the actor, always of the audience; and that, I believe, is the reason why the English text has turned alive under his hands and kindled itself into a veritable poem. It conveys from one language to another the briskness, the brilliance, the eloquence, the spontaneity, the rapture of the original. To me it affords a pleasure that, until this year, I had never hoped to experience, the pleasure of reading an English version of *Cyrano de Bergerac* which could really remind me of the keen delight with which I first read the French original a quarter of a century ago.

CHAPTER 4

The Play in Action

Playing Cyrano

Henry Hewes

In *Cyrano de Bergerac*, one character carries the title
role and the main responsibility of bringing Rostand's work to life. When done correctly, the actor's
rhythms and actions transform words on a page into
a living entity. In this excerpt, theater critic Henry
Hewes reviews the earlier actors who have played
Cyrano. He relates how each actor's mannerisms can
push *Cyrano* toward a polar extreme: entirely intellectual or completely physical. Additionally, various
other critics give their views on whether or not they
judged these interpretations as worthy or unworthy.
Henry Hewes also selected and introduced *Famous
American Plays of the 1940s.*

> This play is nonsense—though the most alluring and be-tinselled
> nonsense ever devised for the theatre. It is untrue to life, experi-
> ence, humanity, human psychology. It sets out to make us
> sorry for a hero with an ungainly nose, a hero who must give
> all his eloquent ardour to a handsome rival and woo his mis-
> tress by proxy. The theme does not hold us for a second out-
> side the theatre. Homely men somehow acquire the prettiest
> wives, and handsome men often mate with quite homely
> women. We see this fact illustrated every day in real life—in
> the streets, in omnibuses, in passing motor-cars, in the apart-
> ment across the street or even next door.

Thus begins a review by my British critical colleague, Alan
Dent, attacking *Cyrano de Bergerac* in good set terms, the occasion being a London revival in 1946 by Tyrone Guthrie
with Ralph Richardson as Cyrano. Objectively considered,
the play itself may merit such an attack, but in the theater
Cyrano's plight attracts and holds us, entertains us, and even
moves us because it is all so romantically stated, scored, and
set, and because it happens in so romantic a period—the
middle of the seventeenth century in the heart of faraway
France. It is sheer—and intensely theatrical—romance, and
the great public has always taken to the stuff for just this rea-

Excerpted from the Afterword, by Henry Hewes, copyright © 1972 by New American
Library, from *Cyrano de Bergerac*, by Edmond Rostand, translated by Lowell Bair.
Used by permission of Dutton Signet, a division of Penguin Putnam, Inc.

son. So have the great critics, with the exception of Bernard Shaw, who was unsusceptible to romance and dismissed it all (as sentiment and worse) as so much "pasteboard." Nevertheless, for most of the more human rest of us, the romance of *Cyrano* is irresistible, however much we may resent the plot's implausibilities.

THE STARRING ROLE

Because of this possibly excessive romanticism and theatricality, the need for proper casting is crucial—especially in the all-important title role, which means more than Hamlet does to *Hamlet*. Since its first production in 1897, *Cyrano* has both tempted and challenged many of the leading actors of America, England, and France. In this country it was a perennial vehicle for the late Walter Hampden, and later was presented successfully on Broadway with José Ferrer (who was also the Cyrano of the film version). In 1962 that fine actor, Christopher Plummer, gave the best performance of his career in Michael Langham's Stratford, Ontario, staging of the classic. Plummer played Cyrano not as a noble-hearted unrequited lover but primarily as a man who cherishes wit, elegance, and the idea of love so much that though his life turns out a failure, his *panache* constitutes a magnificent thumbing of the nose at mortality.

For a perfect understanding of the play, it is necessary to have some understanding of the word "panache," which is actually the last word in the original French. Panache is what Cyrano will carry with him beyond the grave. Literally it is merely the tuft or plume of feathers on an old-style military helmet. But figuratively it is an amalgam of all kinds of dashing qualities—pride, gallantry, swagger, courage, conceit, and conscious superiority. These qualities, moreover, should be genuine and not fake, and should therefore win much more admiration than resentment, and infinitely more trust than distrust.

FRANK LANGELLA

In the summer of 1971, I saw this play at Williamstown, Massachusetts, where it was revived with the splendid young actor, Frank Langella, in the title role. Langella's portrayal emphasized the poetic aspect of Cyrano. He gave us a soft-spoken fellow who compensated for his lack of appeal to the opposite sex by the reputation he knew how to achieve through his daring exploits as a fencer and versifier. From the beginning, this Cyrano never seemed in love with Roxane. Rather he saw in her the opportunity to enjoy the imagined pleasures of a pure and noble sentiment. Indeed, the most emotional moment in this production came when Cyrano suddenly found himself obliged to observe Roxane actually kiss her lover Christian, the handsome nitwit. Langella here made it clear that what was bothering him was not jealousy but an abhorrence for adding physical dimensions to a love he wished to keep a fiction. It was an unusual approach to *Cyrano*, and it proved extremely popular with young audiences with their own drift toward unisexual romanticism.

CHRISTOPHER PLUMMER

Christopher Plummer's 1962 performance at Stratford, Ontario, appeared to me—clear as the nose on his face—superior to all this dazzling actor's other performances. The actor's natural facility—so often inimical to roles that require intense commitment—was here essential to Rostand's quick-witted and dexterous cavalier. But, even more important, Cyrano seemed to allow Plummer to relate many lines and situations to his own world of experience.

This production, adapted and directed by Michael Langham, made this impossibly romantic play convincing and moving by fighting its sentimentality with humor. Here the famous first-act duel was played not simply as a theatrical stunt but rather to reveal to us that for Cyrano the physical task of dueling was a trifle as compared with the mental task of inventing a "ballade" as he went along. (The ballade was an old French form of three eight-line stanzas followed and rounded by a refrain or *envoi* of four lines in the same meter. Rostand's own example from the play will be reproduced when we consider the problems of translation into English.)

The Plummer Cyrano treasured the world of imagination and sensibility. Thus when his opponent, the Vicomte de Valvert, attempted stealthily to kill him while he stood composing with his back turned, Cyrano's deft turn to knock the sword from his opponent's hand just in time was breathtakingly theatrical, yet quintessential of this Cyrano and his governing set of values. He was treating a mortal physical danger with the scornful ease of someone who understands that man's struggle with the real world is a comic business.

And as a comedian, Plummer gave this element welcome. Using his unique ability to go abruptly from internal vulnerability to outrageous clowning without breaking the character's identity, he enjoyed a field day while he was generating "the action." Perhaps his funniest moment came when, after Christian had failed dismally at wooing Roxane on his own, this Cyrano tiptoed up to him and shook his hand in mock-congratulatory hilarity. Plummer's Cyrano seemed to me equally remarkable at creating the inner side of the character's nature. Although Cyrano's oversized nose gives him a grotesque appearance, the actor showed us a man who still dared to hope that Roxane would return his love. When he hears that Roxane turned pale during his duel, he tremblingly asks, "Pale?" and there is a flash of desperate hope in his eyes. A little later he made poignant the hurt of rejection in the conversation with Roxane in which they recall their friendship as children before "adult" realities intruded on fairy-tale imagination.

Best of all, Plummer made the final, hopelessly romantic death-scene work by resisting its sentiment, by meeting death with a certain gaiety, and by arriving at some tough-minded assessments of his life as one in which he was all things—and all in vain. But he smiled as he recalled that he had reached the end of life with his one virtue—his panache—unspotted. While the tone was light and without self-pity, we wept just as helplessly as our grandfathers did at performances we would find ridiculous. Or would we?

That last question must be echoed and repeated by anyone looking back—as I have just been doing—to records of the Cyranos of yesterday and the day-before-yesterday.

WALTER HAMPDEN

The most famous Cyrano in America was that of Walter Hampden, who in four productions between 1923 and 1936 set a world record of playing the role 991 times as compared to Coquelin's 540 times and Richard Mansfield's 380.

Some critics expressed reservations about Hampden's broadsword rather than rapier approach to the role. Percy Hammond in the *New York Tribune* complained for instance that in the duel with Valvert, Hampden "appeared to be more concerned with the fracas itself than with the composition of the famous ballade," so that "you suspected it was not, as he said it was, an improvisation." Nevertheless the *Tribune* critic ultimately admitted that "despite little rifts, we came away believing we had seen a Cyrano. We had had a friendly realization of a man who had 'loved hatred' and a woman, and who had strived his best to displease. A poet and a cynic, a blustering warrior and a dove, and a lovable adventurer who wished to die 'with steel in his heart and laughter on his lips.'"

More enthusiastic still was critic Alan Dale, who explained in the *New York American:*

> Here was a Cyrano who refused the grotesque accessories of Richard Mansfield and whose vocal charm compared with the utterances of the late actor was remarkable. Here was a Cyrano who even obliterated memories of Coquelin. Hampden lacked the dash and the spectacular cynicism of the French actor but he had the more modern embellishment of perfect diction, admirable unstaginess and a delicious neatness of execution. In fact I can recall no finer Cyrano.

Brooks Atkinson, writing about the final 1936 revival, called Hampden's performance ". . . a triumph of conscientious workmanship. The humorous spirit is lacking in his work. It emerges as friskiness. But when the humor is a property of stage exhibition, of show and visual or audible exposition, he knows how to make it count in the theater."

José Ferrer

In 1946 José Ferrer, who like Hampden used the Brian Hooker translation, had a success with Cyrano. Mr. Atkinson wrote: "His Cyrano has a sardonic wit, a strutting style, a bombastic manner of speech and withal a shyness and modesty. For under Rostand's rodomontade this Cyrano has a streak of sadness. Without dimming the purple of Rostand's romantic scheme, Mr. Ferrer has preserved a trace of ordinary human feeling that redeems Cyrano from complete artificiality."

Critic Robert Garland, who had seen the Cyranos of Francis Wilson, Richard Mansfield, Coquelin, Charles Richman, Frank Gilmore, and Walter Hampden, found Ferrer superlative, ". . . bringing the past to life with an amazing mixture of sincerity and bravado."

Actually, Cyrano has always been a remarkable victory of romance and theatricality over true poetry. The British critic of a generation earlier, A. B. Walkely, praised it for being "audaciously, triumphantly, flamboyantly romantic," but pointed out that the play was artifice not art, rhetoric not poetry.

As a kind of crystal-fruit concoction, Ralph Richardson's performance in Tyrone Guthrie's 1946 *Cyrano* was acclaimed. In a BBC broadcast Alan Dent said:

> Richardson plays this superb part probably as well as any Englishman can ever play that intensely French Gascon. He is without the Gallic temperament, of course, the quality that the French themselves call *fougue*. But he has almost everything else that is needed—great vocal range and speed, color, variety and pace, animation when needed and tenderness when called for; a convincing expertness in fencing both with swords and words (and in both at the same time—as in the famous duel to a ballade in the first act). If Ralph Richardson is not particularly like a French actor, it is because, instead of speaking brilliant French verse, he has to speak a translation into English verse that is strained and not particularly brilliant.

COQUELIN, THE ORIGINAL CYRANO

With the advantage of being able to perform in French, the original Cyrano, Coquelin, impressed the foreign critics on his American and British tours of the play. Norman Hapgood in *The Stage in America,* 1897–1900 states enthusiastically:

> Coquelin, who, of course, set the tone for the whole, took the play as a fantasy, a sort of midsummer night's dream, which he read with exquisite taste and a mastery of voice sufficient to give the shades of sadness and humor by the merest touch; the warrior side he simply omitted. Cyrano, as written in the book, is D'Artagnan, poet and wit. Coquelin made him not at all D'Artagnan, moderately a wit, and through and through a poet. . . . It was the literary side of the play to which the cultivated French actor gave the fullest value. He gave each line so lovingly that he seemed unwilling to use it as an excuse for histrionic high relief, preferring to read it perfectly and let it go at that. His Gascon was finely tempered all the time by a fusion and balance of the elements of his nature, moderate when he jested, light when he was sad, treating his own sorrow and the world in general with the docility of a philosopher as well as the sensitiveness of a poet. This understanding of the man and the story naturally fitted some scenes better than others. But Coquelin doubtless calculated every part in view of the whole, and he left at the end a picture poignant and beautiful and lasting, without the full vivacity and volume of the play, but with more beauty of feeling and charm of fantasy than one would be likely to get unassisted from the book.

Hapgood proceeds after this charming summary to describe the performance, scene by scene, in detail. The death scene at the end of the play, in which some other good critics thought that Coquelin failed to be moving, he liked almost more than all the rest: "In the fifth act he became a great actor in the grand style, and thus, ending with his most open and emotional work, fixed his poetic rendering of the play completely in the memory."

A FAILED ATTEMPT

Parenthetically, we may note here that a might-have-been Cyrano de Bergerac on film was Charles Laughton. The idea was projected by no less an impressario than Alexander Korda, and it engaged much of his attention—not to mention that of Charles Laughton, who might easily have been tremendous—for many months in the early thirties. The difficulty, under which the plan faltered and was finally abandoned, was principally due to translation trouble. The English poet Humbert Wolfe was commissioned to do a verse translation. He wrote and eventually published it with a lengthy introduction to explain what trouble he had taken to arrive at a suitable meter for the ears of filmgoers. But the truth is that the poet never did solve his problem, and the film never even reached the studio floor. We shall return in a moment or two to the general problems of translating Rostand into viable English.

FRENCH CYRANOS

In the French theater, since the death of Coquelin we have had two famous and successful Cyranos—that of Pierre Fresnay in 1926 and that of Pierre Dux in 1956. Fresnay we would gladly have seen, as he is still one of the finest actors in Europe. Dux we saw in a delicious production, which was part of a Festival of European Drama, at the Théâtre Sarah Bernhardt. It was the best thing in the whole festival, and Pierre Dux in a curtain speech said he was proud to follow in Coquelin's footsteps.

REVIEWS FOR COQUELIN

Finally, apropos of Coquelin, let me give a taste—no more than a dessert spoonful—of three great English critics whose heyday was roughly that of the actor himself. These are Max Beerbohm, William Archer, and C. E. Montague; and the books from which these passages are taken—*Around Theatres, Study and Stage,* and *Dramatic Values,* respectively— are strongly recommended to all students of the drama.

The Rostand play was the very first which Max Beerbohm covered when he took over from Bernard Shaw in the *Saturday Review* in 1898:

Cyrano will survive because he is practically a new type in drama. I know that the motives of self-sacrifice-in-love and of beauty-adored-by-a-grotesque are as old and as effective as the hills and have been used in literature again and again. I know that self-sacrifice is the motive of most successful plays. But, so far as I know, beauty-adored-by-a-grotesque has never been used with the grotesque as stage-hero. At any rate it has never been used so finely and so tenderly as by M. Rostand, whose hideous swashbuckler with the heart of gold and talent for improvising witty or beautiful verses is far too novel, I think, and too convincing and too attractive not to be permanent. . . . Even if anyone does not like the play, it will be something, hereafter, to be able to bore one's grandchildren by telling them about Coquelin as Cyrano.

William Archer also enjoyed the play and performance hugely. Though wondering rather, in the middle of his splendid essay, why he, "a canny Scot, born at the spiritual antipodes of Gascony, should rejoice in it with exceeding great joy," he wholeheartedly concludes:

It is surely beyond all question that many of the scenes, and almost all the great speeches, gain by the extraordinary brilliancy of M. Coquelin's action and delivery. It is said that he is not sincere, not pathetic enough: he would be out of the picture were he more so. We do not want realism, we want fantasy, even in the scenes of passion and pathos. The whole fabric is artificial, and an absolutely real hero would tear it to shreds. There would have been no harm, I take it, in a more picturesque and perhaps an uglier Cyrano. M. Coquelin in all he does, is dapper rather than flamboyant. But his diction was unsurpassable. In the scenes of tenderness and melancholy it had all the sincerity that consists with this particular literary form. The part, as I have said, is a bravura part; virtuosity is what it chiefly demands; but both author and actor are as sincere as they can be, considering how diabolically clever they are. In the last act I thought M. Coquelin genuinely moving.

Lastly, Montague in Manchester, wrote:

In his mouth the French dramatic couplet, that stumbling block of English youth, was a thing transfigured. Not that its own build and movement, so joltsome or jig-jog to some foreign ears, were disguised. They were revelled in, joyously championed. He practised on the verse a kind of double magic. First he shed over the stiff-seeming lines such color, diversity, warmth, colloquial quickness, that hearers, to whom these French Alexandrines had seemed to fall far short of human vivacity, half wondered whether perhaps the use of rhymed couplets was what human speech, in its longing for heightened expression at crises of feeling, had really been groping for always till now. How apt a fire they had, in Coquelin's mouth, to Cyrano's burning love. In the great speech below Roxane's window, clause sprang out of clause and line flowed into line with a kind of passionate logic; the way every phrase was given made some place in your mind ache to be filled by the next. And yet—other half of the magic—all the metrical and rhythmic structure of Rostand's verse, or of Molière's, was there. Its stately march was beaten out, like some steadying and fortifying bass, behind the more free and various melody of the eager spoken word.

The rarest of Coquelin's powers comes next—the sheer comic force with which he embraced and enjoyed the idea of what he was acting. The communicable energy of his joy in all the contents of human nature was incomparable; no comedian in our time has glowed with a more radiant heat of life and delight.

REJECTION OF VERSE

Montague's remarks on the difficulties of rhymed verse in the English theater and on the art with which a good actor like Coquelin could make it not only tolerable but delectable in the French language point up the crucial importance of proper translation—as well as casting—to this play. There have hitherto been three well-known English translations of *Cyrano de Bergerac:* one by Stuart Ogilvie and Louis N. Parker, another by Gladys Thomas and Mary F. Guillemard, and a third by Brian Hooker. All three versions were in blank verse or in rhymed verse which could echo only fleetingly the music of the original. Now comes the version by Lowell Blair to which these notes act as an Afterword. Mr. Blair seems to me to have wisely avoided rhyme almost entirely and to have been content to give a straightforward translation, free but not too free, and almost entirely in prose. (How it acts in the theater, of course, only can be determined by a stage production.) An appreciative taste for blank verse (unrhymed)—even in its subtlest form, as in late Shakespeare—comes to most of us before we have left our first school. But the relish of dramatic verse in the form of rhymed couplets—the style prevailing in the French classic drama of Racine and Corneille and even in the more serious comedies of Molière—is an acquired taste. And, if the truth must be told, many playgoers of forty and over have spent half their lives trying to acquire it—and not always succeeding.

From Stage to Silver Screen

Jeanne-Marie Zeck

Over the years, movies have usurped the theater's role in popular culture, offering frequently rotated, wide-ranging selections. Consequently, it's not surprising that at least four *Cyrano*-related movie adaptations exist. Jeanne-Marie Zeck examines the relationship of two modern films—*Roxanne* and *The Truth About Cats and Dogs*—that seem to derive their basic concepts from *Cyrano de Bergerac*. Adapting *Cyrano* to film, in these instances, offers opportunities to tailor the story to today's audience by letting the film address current social issues such as gender roles and eating disorders. Zeck is a visiting assistant professor of English at Susquehanna University and the coauthor of two plays, *Welcome Home* and *In the Heart of the Hills*.

Within a period of nine years, film audiences have enjoyed three adaptations of Edmond Rostand's play *Cyrano de Bergerac*. In 1987 Steve Martin's film *Roxanne* delighted audiences; in 1990 Jean-Paul Rappeneau's *Cyrano de Bergerac* won favor with Gerard Depardieu in the title role; in 1996 Audrey Wells produced her delightful screenplay *The Truth about Cats and Dogs* that switches the sexes of the three protagonists and, by doing so, raises important social issues. The production of these three films suggests that Rostand's play is a rich expression of the confusion of love, the frustration and fears lovers encounter when dealing with one another, and the hope for that which is nearly impossible— true love. *Cyrano de Bergerac* is a story about longing for a lover and about the fear of being found unworthy by the beloved. It is also a tale about a hero who possesses extraordinary intelligence, wit, charm, courage, and, of course,

Excerpted from "Stumbling Toward Ecstasy: *Cyrano de Bergerac* as Comedy in Martin's *Roxanne* and Wells's *The Truth About Cats and Dogs*, by Jeanne-Marie Zeck, *Literature/Film Quarterly*, vol. 27, no. 3 (1999), pp. 218–22. Reprinted with permission.

panache. For more than 300 years, audiences of all kinds, including readers of history, theatergoers, and movie aficionados, have been fascinated by Cyrano's tale. Edmond Rostand found inspiration for his play in the life of seventeenth-century Frenchman, Savinien Cyrano de Bergerac, who was the epitome of the Renaissance Man. . . .

Two and a half centuries later, Edmond Rostand resurrected this hero by fictionalizing his life in *Cyrano de Bergerac*, the romantic tragedy written in rhymed Alexandrine verse. In 1897 the play opened to an audience hungry for romance, hungry for hope, and hungry for a noble hero. Rostand's play became an instant classic. Patricia Elliott Williams argues that the play is a classic not simply for its presentation of a clever, bold, swashbuckling hero, but largely because it fulfills the six Aristotelian characteristics of tragedy: plot, character, thought, spectacle, diction, and music. The play's longevity, then, can be attributed to Rostand's fine craftsmanship: his coherent, compelling action, morally sound and substantive characters, poetic language, and theatricality.

FILM ADAPTATIONS

Of the three film adaptations to appear in the last decade, Jean-Paul Rappeneau's film is the most faithful to the tragic tone and original style of Rostand's script. Many of the scenes are literally dark—in the theater, in the streets, below Roxane's balcony. Brilliant but aggressive, Cyrano moves through the action ostracizing and isolating himself from most human company. A witty man with the soul of a poet, he inspires both respect and fear. The tender lover only rarely appears in Rappeneau's film, and the humor carries an edge as sharp as Cyrano's sword.

Steve Martin's 1987 adaptation *Roxanne* and Audrey Wells's 1996 film *The Truth about Cats and Dogs* update the play to make it accessible to contemporary audiences. Most significantly, both Martin and Wells transform the dark romantic tragedy into pithy romantic comedy. These American films entertain and teach. In the original play, the hero succumbs to death thereby ending the conflict, but not resolving it. After all, Roxane must live on, knowing that she has lost her great love not once, but twice. The American screenwriters favor survival over tragic death. In the comedies, the characters work through the deception to the difficult and awkward confrontation. The protagonists learn to understand and forgive one another, laugh at themselves, and move toward intimacy; these are essential skills and lessons for those engaged in contemporary romantic relationships.

By closely adhering to Rostand's script, Martin's film achieves a satisfying cohesion that is strengthened by ingenious changes. In his article, "American Cinematic Adaptations of *Cyrano de Bergerac*," Don Kunz notes that "Martin and Schepisi obviously have taken great care to make this film adaptation a coherent re-creation in which revised and invented material are smoothly integrated into an appropriate conceptual framework." Martin's adherence to Rostand's original play proves that Aristotle's six elements of tragedy are also conducive to comedy.

Roxanne takes place in the mid-1980s in the fictitious town of Nelson, Colorado. Filmed in British Columbia, the film takes full advantage of stunningly beautiful scenery. Aristotle might define as *spectacle* shots of the mountains and the snug little town in the midst of a perfect summer. Steve Martin plays the Cyrano character, Charlie D. Bales (Charlie and Cyrano share the same initials). Like his literary counterpart, Charlie has a great deal of panache. Rostand describes this as a spiritual strength and grace, a sense of overriding courage with a bit of danger thrown in. While Martin's protagonist has the soul and wit of the original Cyrano, he forgoes the anti-social characteristics and resorts to violence only when ruthlessly harassed for his enormous nose. Martin moves away from violence toward more affirming activity when he makes Charlie a patient fire chief in charge of a hilariously inept crew rather than the leader of a group of military cadets. Charlie and his men are meant to prevent or limit tragedy rather than participate in it and contribute to it, as soldiers must. Martin introduces Chris (the Christian character) as a handsome young man who comes to help Charlie train his crew.

A CHANGED ROXANE

Martin makes another noteworthy change from the original script when he names the film after Roxanne. Rather than merely being Charlie's object of desire, Roxanne becomes an entity in herself, a subject rather than an object. She exhibits intelligence, depth, a sense of humor, of purpose, and of justice. The expansion of Roxanne's role answers Aristotle's requirement of a three-dimensional, consistent, and morally sound *character.* Anthony Burgess, in the introduction to his own adaptation of Rostand's play, registers this complaint: "Of all the characters, the least satisfactory to a modern audience is Roxane." Martin remedies this problem with the significant addition of a career for Roxanne Kowalski, played by Daryl Hannah. She is an astronomy graduate student on the verge of the "career-making" discovery of a comet. This contemporary Roxanne is a heroine in her own right and a worthy partner for the hero.

Ingeniously, Martin incorporates Rostand's use of astronomy into his own script by making Roxanne a scientist. Her *diction* often includes astronomical terms that she defines while Charlie and the audience interpret them as romantic metaphors. Roxanne's profession as an astronomer pays off nicely through humor as well as poetry. Before pursuing Roxanne, Chris talks with Charlie and tries to raise his own self-confidence by saying, "Why am I so nervous to talk with her? She's no rocket scientist." Setting straight the somewhat dimwitted Chris, Charlie remarks, "Actually, she *is* a rocket scientist." Not only is the line a clever use of a common phrase, but it indicates that Charlie is respectful and appreciative of Roxanne while Chris is oblivious to all but her beauty.

LESS VIOLENCE

Occasionally Martin reverses Rostand's play: instead of having the Cyrano and Christian characters leave town by going to war, he keeps the men stationary. Roxanne leaves to continue her research at the university. Her discovery of a comet is a benign and lovely addition to human knowledge, rather than a violent act of defense and destruction. By focusing on such accomplishments Martin again promotes life-affirming actions; he also successfully develops Roxanne's character to reveal a serious, intelligent scientist—a woman of substance and spirit.

Steve Martin's ingenious additions and changes enhance Rostand's original script resulting in a plot that contains an Aristotelian sense of *complete action:* small and large events pay off beautifully as the film moves forward. When he is publicly insulted in a bar, Charlie challenges the rude stranger to a duel of wits. With great panache and self-deprecating humor, Charlie launches into a litany of twenty clever insults for the bearer of an enormous nose including, "You must love the little birdies so to give them this to perch on." Several scenes later, Charlie is seated at his desk, writing a love letter to Roxanne. As the camera circles him we see, perched on his nose, a little finch. Not only is the image a physicalization of Charlie's clever line in the bar (taken directly from Rostand), but the bird perched contentedly on his nose also suggests Charlie's nature: he is a gentle man.

A RICHLY TEXTURED STORY

In the film's final scene, two earlier scenes are evoked; this, too, contributes to a sense of *complete action*. As the film

A MODERN CYRANO

In Roxanne, *a movie based on Rostand's* Cyrano de Bergerac, *the character C.D. plays a modern Cyrano. C.D., also an intellectual, regards an unimaginative insult, "big nose," as a failing to equal ugliness. This excerpt is his demonstration, which parallels Cyrano's in the play (Act 1, Scene 4), of how to really insult a nose.*

C. D.   All right. . . . Here goes. Let's start with . . . Obvious: Is that your nose or did a bus park on your face? Meteorological: Everybody take cover. She's going to blow. Sad: Oh, why the long face? Deductive: With an eraser like that, there must be a mighty big pencil around here somewhere. Helpful: If you got some handles for that thing, you'd have a nice set of luggage. *(With a lisp, moving to the bar.)* Fashionable: You know, it might deemphasize your nose if you wore something larger, like Wyoming. Snide: Table for two? Personal: Well, here we are, just the three of us. Punctual: All right, Delman, your nose was on time, but *you* were fifteen minutes late! Instructive: No, you've got it wrong: Let a *smile* be your umbrella. Envious: Oh, I wish I were you! To be able to smell your own ear. *(Moves to Roxanne's table.)* Naughty: Pardon me sir, some of the ladies have asked if you'd mind putting that thing away. . . . Philosophical: You know, it's not the size of a nose that's important, it's what's in it that matters. . . . Humorous: Laugh and the world laughs with you; sneeze and it's good-bye Seattle. Commercial: Hi, I'm Earl Scheib and I can paint that nose for thirty-nine ninety-five. . . . Polite: Would mind not bobbing your head; the orchestra keeps changing tempo. Melodic: *(singing)* He's got the whole world, in his nose. . . . Sympathetic: What happened? Did your parents lose a bet with God? . . . Complimentary: you must *love* the little birdies to give them this to perch on. . . .

Steve Martin, *Roxanne.* New York: Grove Press, 1987.

ends, Charlie sits on the roof of his house and muses. Just as Roxanne's status as a contemporary American woman allows her to travel and pursue a career, so it allows her to pursue her lover. When Roxanne comes to forgive his deception and woo him, her location on the ground and his on the roof remind the audience of the balcony/window scene in which Charlie and Chris together win Roxanne's affection. In the final scene the positions of the lovers are reversed and Chris's presence no longer interferes with a true expression of admiration and love.

The final scene also has another precedent: Midway through the film, Charlie displays his skills as a fire chief and sensitive human being when he is sent to rescue an overweight boy who isolates himself on a rooftop. Immediately Charlie recognizes that the boy does not require a physical rescue, but an emotional one. Empathizing with the child who has been harassed for his physical appearance, Charlie joins him. Side by side on the roof, the two of them relax into a melancholy, thoughtful solitude. Later when Roxanne comes to save Charlie, her rescue is emotional as well: She saves him from isolation and depression by assuring him of her love. Such building of images and themes results in a richly layered, textured story in which every moment resonates.

In this romantic comedy the characters answer the demands of Aristotle: They are well-rounded, coherent, and believable. Charlie and Roxanne exhibit their moral goodness in self-sacrifice and forgiveness, respectively. The thought processes and actions of each protagonist are consistent. Charlie's unique diction is most evident in his humorous assaults and love letters, while Roxanne displays a professional diction with her use of astronomical terms and a personal diction in her poetic wooing of Charlie in the final scene. Spectacle is utilized well on location in the mountains of British Columbia; music augments the moods and humor of the movie. Finally, Rostand's poignant *catharsis* is replaced by joyful resolution when Charlie and Roxanne finally unite.

ROLE REVERSAL

The most recent of the three contemporary film adaptations of Rostand's play is Audrey Wells's *The Truth about Cats and Dogs*. Although the film is based loosely on his play, no credit is given to Rostand. While a feminist filmmaker may be wise to avoid adhering to the ancient patriarchal Aristotelian elements of drama, there is no evidence that Wells seeks to create a new feminist structure upon which to build substantial women's films. As a result, the film lacks a cogent plot. Yet Wells introduces important themes when she reverses the sexes of the protagonists. The Cyrano character is Dr. Abby Barnes (played by Janeane Garofalo), a skillful and compassionate veterinarian and violinist. Although she is witty, talented, and soulful, Abby, like Cyrano, feels that she cannot measure up to her culture's definition of physical beauty. Her counterpart in the Christian role is Noelle, played by Uma Thurman, a tall, slender blonde who "can literally stop traffic." Brian, a handsome English photographer (played by Ben Chaplin), takes the role of a masculine Roxane who is pursued by the women in tandem.

While the film lacks the cohesion of its predecessors, there is much to recommend it. Janeane Garofalo as Abby Barnes is a wonderful comic talent with an affable delivery. The character of Abby is well-developed and disarming. More believable and more compelling than the love story is the developing friendship between the two women. They live in the same apartment building and meet one evening. Abby is playing her violin when she hears a man abusing his girlfriend. Rushing to the rescue, violin bow in hand, she accosts Noelle's boyfriend with more wit than he can handle. When Roy leaves, Noelle explains to her neighbor why she stays with him: "You've gotta have a boyfriend, don't you? Otherwise it's just you and your cat and pretty soon there are 40 candles on your birthday cake." Despite the advantage of her physical beauty, Noelle suffers from low self-esteem; consequently, she accepts an abusive relationship.

SOCIAL IMPLICATIONS

Juliann Garey of *Glamour* magazine calls the film "a savvy, pointed and hilarious commentary on the politics of beauty." Wells's film introduces significant issues, including women's self-esteem and eating disorders. Noelle is a model suffering from anorexia. She asks Abby, "Do you believe that you are what you eat? See, that's what scares me because I look good on the outside but on the inside there's nothing." Noelle comments that Abby, on the other hand, is "rich." Abby is short and, by contemporary mainstream standards, overweight. Insecurity about her weight prevents her from actively pursuing Brian. The theme of intellectual and spiritual substance versus physical beauty (which will attract the handsome photographer?) is woven throughout the film. Noelle's hunger is a metaphor that expresses her longing for recognition and acceptance. She is literally starving for approbation. The conversation between Noelle and Abby resonates in a later scene when Brian feeds Noelle an entire plate of rich cakes. Noelle relishes every bite; the scene is dense with sexual overtones. But Noelle's earlier admission of her hunger marks the cake-eating scene as more poignant than sensuous.

In Rostand's play, Roxane crosses enemy lines to bring food to her husband Christian and the other starving soldiers. In Wells's screenplay, Brian (in the Roxane role) brings food to his starving lover, Noelle (who plays the Christian role). However, the food he brings is insubstantial fluff. Likewise Brian's affection is insubstantial fluff because it is motivated only by sexual attraction. In truth, Brian loves Abby, not Noelle.

Audrey Wells's choice of weight as the central issue for the female protagonists is especially appropriate and timely. In contemporary American culture, young women suffer from anorexia, bulimia, and other eating disorders in epidemic numbers. Anorexia can be interpreted as a symptom of a misogynous culture: Insistence on thinness as a prerequisite for beauty suggests that the less of a woman there is, the better.

Being thin and beautiful, Noelle has the opportunity to claim Brian for her own; he leads her up to his bedroom. Instead, she pursues her friendship with Abby, apologizing for her momentary indiscretion. Here the film features a montage, as many romantic comedies do. However, in Wells's film, the montage focuses on the relationship between Noelle and Abby. This shift in focus from the heterosexual romantic relationship to an intimate women's friendship is noteworthy: This is where the real soul of the film lies. Noelle actively pursues her friend through a series of phone messages. Abby listens, but refuses to respond. Noelle is in the midst of learning an important lesson about substantive relationships: She begins to value herself and a woman friend. Abby and Noelle achieve a level of intimacy and respect that is absent from the male-female romantic relationships in the film. Yet the movie ends when Brian realizes

Abby's worth. He utters the original Roxane's sentiments when he tells Abby that he has only loved one woman, and he does not want to lose her twice. The two sit on a park bench overlooking the ocean and kiss as the sun sets. Unfortunately, Audrey Wells abandons the alternative storyline: the deep, rich, intimate relationship between the two women and chooses to focus on the more acceptable, predictable heterosexual union.

AN INCOMPLETE WORK

Although the themes of self-esteem, domestic violence, eating disorders, and women's friendships are raised, Wells fails to explore them thoroughly. Yet these are the issues that could have transformed this pleasant comedy into a consistent, substantial, and satisfying film. In an interview, Uma Thurman claimed that the movie is "supposed to be a subversive feminist comedy." Unfortunately, it does not go far enough; it isn't bold enough. Wells's screenplay falls short of success because it lacks a cogent plot and fails to follow through with its feminist ideals. This film is a lesson in lost opportunities. Viewers may miss the more compelling aspects of the film and determine that *The Truth about Cats and Dogs* is, as *Rolling Stone* reviewer Peter Travers states, "a perfunctory romantic comedy."

Edmond Rostand's play written in 1897 resonates a century later when each of the three contemporary film adaptations offers audiences a hero who knows that life, with all its challenges, requires a great deal of panache. Rappeneau, Martin, and Wells remind audiences of the lessons of the play: love is awkward; lovers are flawed. And yet, love is all the richer for the humanity and generosity, the wit, intelligence, and diversity it embraces. Each script suggests that loving the self is the first step toward intimacy and compassion. The fact that there have been three adaptations of Rostand's play in nine years speaks to the charm, truth, and timelessness of the original story. The American comedies suggest the importance of survival, the necessity of pursuing love through confusions and difficulties, and the ultimate importance of forgiveness.

A Review of *Cyrano de Bergerac*, the Movie (1990)

Roger Ebert

Roger Ebert, well-known film critic for television and for the *Chicago Sun-Times*, discusses the importance and results of effective casting in Jean-Paul Rappeneau's 1990 film version of *Cyrano de Bergerac*. Gerard Depardieu, now perhaps as recognizable as his predecessor José Ferrer in the part of Cyrano, proves his mettle in a virtuoso performance. Depardieu might not fit the part's physical requisites; nevertheless, the claim that Cyrano epitomizes the French nation finds some validation as this truly French actor pushes the play to its limits.

It is entirely appropriate that Cyrano—whose very name evokes the notion of grand romantic gestures—should have lived his life bereft of romance. What is romanticism, after all, but a bold cry about how life should be, not about how it is? And so here is Cyrano de Bergerac, hulking, pudding-faced, with a nose so large he is convinced everyone is laughing at him—yet he dares to love the fair Roxane. I have made it one of my rules in life never to have anything to do with anyone who does not instinctively love Cyrano, and I am most at home with those who identify with him.

The "real" Cyrano, if there was such a creature beneath the many layers of myth that have grown up around the name, lived in France from 1619 to 1655, and wrote stories about his magnificent voyages to the moon and the sun. He inspired the Cyrano we love, a more modern creation, the work of Edmond Rostand, who wrote a play in 1897 that may not have been great literature, but has captured the imagination of everyone who has read it, and has been recycled countless times.

Steve Martin and Daryl Hannah starred in the wonderful modern-dress comedy *Roxanne* (1987), inspired by the outlines of Rostand's story, and now here is a magnificently lusty, brawling, passionate and tempestuous classical version, directed by Jean-Paul Rappeneau. Cyrano is played by Gerard Depardieu, the most popular actor in France, who won the best actor award at the Cannes Film Festival last May.

You would not think he would be right for the role. Shouldn't Cyrano be smaller, more tentative, more pathetic —instead of this outsized, physically confident man of action? Depardieu is often said to be "wrong" for his roles. His physical presence makes a definite statement on the screen, and then his acting genius goes to work, and transforms him into whatever is required for the role—into a spiritual priest, a hunchbacked peasant, a medieval warrior, a car salesman, a businessman, a sculptor, a gangster.

Here he plays Cyrano, gadfly and rabble-rouser, man about town, friend of some, envied by many, despised by a powerful few, and hopelessly, oh, most painfully and endearingly, in love with Roxane (Anne Brochet). But his nose is too large. Not quite as long as Steve Martin's was, perhaps, but long enough that when he looks in the mirror he knows it would be an affront to present the nose anywhere in the vicinity of the fair Roxane with an amorous purpose attached to it.

THE FOIL

Now here is the inoffensive clod Christian de Neuvillette (Vincent Perez), Cyrano's friend. He is a romantic, too, but not in Cyrano's league. For him, love is a fancy. For Cyrano, a passion. Yet if Cyrano cannot have Roxane, then he will help his friend, and so he ghostwrites letters and ghost-recites speeches in the moonlight, and because Roxane senses that the words come from a heart brave and true, she pledges herself to Christian. The irony—which only the audience can fully appreciate—is that anyone with a heart so pure that she could love a cheesy lump like Christian because of his language could certainly love a magnificent man like Cyrano for the same reason, and regardless of his nose.

The screenplay by Rappeneau and the skilled veteran Jean-Claude Carriere spins this love story in a web of court intrigue and scandal, with Cyrano deeply involved on the wrong (that is, the good) side. And all leads up to the heartbreaking final round of revelations and truth-telling, and at last to Depardieu's virtuoso dying scene, which has to be seen to be believed.

What other actor would have had the courage to go with such determination so far over the top, to milk the pathos so shamelessly, to stagger and groan and weep and moan until it would all be funny? Only the French could conceive and write, and perhaps only Depardieu could deliver, a dying speech that rises and falls with pathos and defiance for so long, only to end with the assertion that when he is gone, he will be remembered for . . . what? His heart? Courage? No, of course not. Nothing half so commonplace: For his panache.

A BELIEVABLE CLASSIC

Cyrano de Bergerac is a splendid movie not just because it tells its romantic story, and makes it visually delightful, and centers it on Depardieu, but for a better reason: The movie acts as if it believes this story. Depardieu is not a satirist—not here, anyway. He plays Cyrano on the level, for keeps.

Of course, the material is comic. But it is the frequent mistake of amateurs to play comedy for laughs, when the great artists know there is only one way to play it, and that is very seriously indeed. But with panache.

France's War of the Noses: Dueling Cyranos of Stage and Screen

Pascal Privat and Benjamin Ivry

Whether viewed on stage or in film, *Cyrano de Bergerac* has consistently formed an intimate connection with the French people. *Cyrano* offers its audience a hero and a rebirth of romance—no small contributions—and France has responded by making the play its most performed drama. In this excerpt from *Newsweek,* Pascal Privat and Benjamin Ivry note the close relationship that exists between Rostand's play and French society and observe how the former provides the latter with an intrinsically French role model and fuel for a renewed sense of nationalism.

It made Catherine Deneuve burst into tears. It made Paris's toughest film critics break into applause. It made France's prime minister purr with pleasure. *It* is director Jean-Paul Rappeneau's lavish $20 million production of "Cyrano de Bergerac," starring Gérard Depardieu as the verse-spinning soldier with the gigantic nose. "A real film, a great one!" Le Monde gushed after the première last month. The film has been selling out at Paris cinemas ever since, but movie buffs aren't alone in going berserk over Bergerac. At the Théatre Marigny near the Champs-Elysées, an equally grandiose stage production with an equally big star—Jean-Paul Belmondo—is sold out through September. Small wonder: "Cyrano," said the daily Libération, "is France's No. 1 hero."

The play is France's most performed piece of drama. Since it was first produced in 1897, Cyrano has been staged everywhere from Shanghai to Staten Island; counting Rappeneau's version, it has now been turned into seven films—

including the memorable 1987 "Roxanne," directed by Fred Schepisi and starring Steve Martin. That's quite impressive for a work most theater scholars say isn't very good in the first place. It is long and arduous; for the role of Cyrano alone, an actor must memorize 1,400 lines of alexandrine verse. Its 17th-century historical context is obscure. And its plot is silly: Cyrano, a witty but ugly officer, loves the beautiful Roxane, who in turn is enamored with the handsome but dumb Christian de Neuvillette. Cyrano selflessly arms Christian with poetic speeches and letters that help him woo Roxane. Then Christian dies in battle, and Roxane retires to a convent. Cyrano waits 15 years to confess that he was the real author of Christian's verse. Stunned by the revelation, Roxane falls in love with Cyrano. But it's too late: Cyrano dies. The End.

NATIONAL LEGEND

Such weaknesses notwithstanding, Cyrano is a great role with a quintessentially French quality—the character has panache. "He is a great fighter. He's a thug who wants to say 'I love you,'" says Depardieu. "I'm proud to be French when I see 'Cyrano'." Belmondo puts it this way: "Cyrano represents France, with its Don Quixote side, fighting against anything and everything, ready to attack great powers, even society itself."

"Cyrano" became a national legend the first night it opened: author Edmond Rostand was awarded the Legion of Honor before the final curtain even fell. Today, "Cyrano's" symbolic stature in French society is still so powerful that some scholars debate who among France's modern politicians can measure up to Monsieur de Bergerac. Charles de Gaulle is a frequently mentioned contender, but his detractors counter that the only trait shared by the two heroes is the size of their noses.

For the moment, the French seem more concerned with which actor is winning the War of the Noses—Depardieu or Belmondo. Depardieu's masterful blend of strength and vulnerability may tilt the balance in his favor; the magazine Paris Match said that the part propelled him into the pantheon of French cinema next to Jean Gabin, the legendary star of the '30s. To be fair, Depardieu, 41, benefits greatly from the magnificence of the film, which is scheduled to open in the United States this Christmas. It would be hard to look bad amid 2,000 actors and extras, 300 kinds of costumes, 40 sets inspired by Rembrandt and Vermeer, a man-made forest and a screenplay adroitly streamlined to a digestible 135 minutes by Jean-Claude Carrière.

Not that the Marigny stage production—45 actors, five sets—is shabby. Critics found little to fault in Belmondo's athletic performance other than that his monstrous proboscis—crafted by a former makeup man of de Gaulle's—was just too exaggerated. But enthusiastic theatergoers don't seem to mind: at the end of one recent performance, they leaped from their seats as Belmondo tossed the latex schnoz into the audience. The acclaim is no small victory for the 57-year-old actor who was the heartthrob of French New Wave cinema. Long ago, Belmondo was warned against aspiring to classic parts. "Jean-Paul," advised his drama teacher at the *Comédie Française,* "I'm afraid you'll never be able to play leading-man roles."

CHAPTER 5

Reception and Criticism

READINGS ON
CYRANO DE BERGERAC

Mixed Reception of *Cyrano de Bergerac*

W.L. Parker

Decades after its initial opening, *Cyrano de Bergerac* retains its ability to draw audiences. Writing in 1931 in his critical commentary of Helen Dole's translation of *Cyrano*, W.L. Parker conveys the difficulty of critiquing a work whose popular success is already determined. However, Rostand's literary status was not as solid and was a frequent topic of debate. Most critics agree that *Cyrano* is a beautiful work, but the question remains of whether or not it can be called a classic piece of literature. W.L. Parker contributed commentary to other works including *The Fables of Aesop; The Three Cuckolds, out of Chaucer;* and *Aphrodite (Ancient Matters)*.

The critic of literature has no more difficult task than that of appraising properly a work that has achieved current success to an eminent degree. Such a work needs no interpreter or introducer, because it has already introduced itself. It does not lend itself readily to calm judgment, both because the critic is liable to be influenced by the same enthusiasm that has affected the general public, and because, on the other hand, if he has not been so influenced, he is likely to be overanxious to prove his own independence, and is thus in danger of becoming captious and unjust. Yet it is obvious that if there be any good in criticism, successful authors, who presumably will become still greater public benefactors, ought to get the benefit of it, while the reader who is in danger of being misled by his enthusiasm should be set straight at once. Hence contemporary criticism of all books, successful or unsuccessful, is practically indispensable, and hence it is that even *Cyrano de Bergerac*, fascinating though it be, cannot escape the common fate of being weighed in the balance.

Excerpted from the Critical Commentary, by W.L. Parker, in *Cyrano de Bergerac*, by Edmond Rostand, translated by Helen B. Dole (Cleveland: World, 1931).

CONFLICTING VIEWS

That it should have tipped the balance in both directions since its production was to be expected. It was welcomed with a warmth which probably neither its talented author, M. Edmond Rostand, nor its chief actor, M. Coquelin, fully anticipated; it was translated for foreign readers and adapted to foreign stages; it was pronounced a masterpiece by critics of established repute. But less flattering opinions were also heard. Here in America, Norman Hapgood did not hesitate to declare that the drama was to him "on the stage what it had been in the reading,—an extremely clever proof of skill, a brilliant show of execution, a series of scenes exactly calculated to exhibit the powers of a strong and versatile French actor,—all this, but without simplicity, inevitableness, deep sincerity, without, in short, any true greatness." Mr. Stanley Young asserted that "not even Shakespeare has given us a hero that appeals to us as Cyrano," and that if we "search the whole range of Corneille, Racine, Molière, Victor Hugo, or any other French dramatist," we shall "find nothing on a higher level." Which of these two judgments is the correct one, or does not experience teach us rather that neither judgment is likely to be entirely correct and that we shall do well to seek a safe stand between them?

The important question is whether M. Rostand has succeeded in writing a great play. As we have seen, the public, everywhere, and a large number of critics think that he has. A few bold critics maintain that he has not, and a few readers, not so bold, discreetly hold their tongues. If numbers are to count in such a matter, M. Rostand's case is won—his play is the chief contribution to dramatic literature that has been made for many years.

THE PLAY'S FLAWS

Now, plainly, the opinion of the majority ought to count in such a matter, and just as plainly, the objections that can be raised against the drama should have a respectful hearing. But what are these objections? This question may be answered somewhat as follows:—

The play is called a "heroic comedy," yet it degenerates almost to opera bouffe in the fourth act, which also embraces a tragic element in the death of Christian, while the fifth act is filled with sentimental romance—the very last element a true comedy ought to contain. Again, Cyrano is the only character who is a distinct person, and one person with many personages cannot furnish sufficient play of character to equip a great comedy. Comedy there is in certain scenes,— as, for example, in the fifth scene of the third act, in which Christian fails so egregiously to make the proper sort of love to Roxane,—but the suggestion of romantic melodrama is never far removed. In other words, the play seems to be a good deal of a hybrid, to lack the essential unity of a true work of art. On the other hand, viewed merely as a piece of

---

THE PLAY'S APPEAL

Critics Jay B. Hubbell and John O. Beaty, in An Introduction to Drama, *assert that Cyrano's universal appeal as a hero helps compensate for his flaws. Additionally, they argue that* Cyrano de Bergerac's *effectiveness on the stage transforms disparate elements into a great play.*

Rostand's masterpiece is *Cyrano de Bergerac* (1897). This poetic drama, the hero of which is an almost forgotten French author, was written for and around the famous actor Coquelin. The play has wit, charm, poetry, and theatrical effectiveness; but it lacks consistency of characterization, even in the case of the hero. Each act is very effective in itself, but the five acts do not make a consistent, well-proportioned whole. Nevertheless *Cyrano* is one of the finest of all contemporary plays and is not unworthy of the tradition of Corneille, whose heroic plays it sometimes recalls. The fundamental idea of the play is excellent. Cyrano is a poet, a soldier, an accomplished duelist, a romantic lover; but he is hideously ugly, for his nose is so large as to seem a personal deformity. On the Elizabethan stage Cyrano might have been the butt of ridicule, but he appeals to the sentiment that lies back of the story of the ugly duckling. Those of us who are not beautiful or handsome are likely to endow ourselves, by way of compensation, with other attractive qualities. On the stage the sharp contrast between extreme ugliness and greatness of soul is startlingly effective. Cyrano, however, is, for all his charm, a bundle of fine points for the actor rather than a living man like [Shakespeare's] Hamlet or Falstaff. And yet on the stage the play is so effective that we are swept off our feet and our critical faculties are paralyzed. *Cyrano*, if not a great tragedy, is, in spite of its faults, one of the best of contemporary plays.

Jay B. Hubbell and John O. Beaty, *An Introduction to Drama.* New York: The Macmillan Company, 1927.

literature, it may be described with some reason as a clever rather than a truly witty or humorous performance, and as being fuller of charm than of compelling power. It amuses us and delights us, but it appeals to the fancy much more than to the imagination, and it furnishes us with little of that "criticism of life" which Matthew Arnold has taught us to demand from all poetry that challenges our admiration. This may, indeed, seem to be a rigorous test to apply to such a play, but after all *Cyrano de Bergerac* is poetic drama, and its admirers have applied to it terms of praise hitherto confined to the world's few indisputable masterpieces.

THE PLAY'S STRENGTHS

It is now time, however, to consider some of the things that may be said in favor of the play. In the first place, it is certainly most effective. It interests spectator or reader, and fills him with a sympathy which purges him of selfishness and low emotions. It is impossible not to be drawn to Cyrano; we pity his misfortunes and admire his self-abnegation. Our critical judgment may tell us that M. Rostand is not the first dramatist to present his hero as an exemplar of almost superhuman self-sacrifice, but we must confess that he has on the whole succeeded remarkably well in the task he set himself. It may not have been a fit task for a comic dramatist, but its accomplishment at least shows distinguished power and an unusual comprehension of the demands of the theatergoing public of the present day, which, weary of realism, has been glad to get back to romantic drama. The historical setting of the play is excellent, and the invention displayed in its construction is worthy of high praise. M. Rostand may not have given us enough of the higher side of the real Cyrano, he may have subordinated philosophy to sentiment, but surely no one save a born dramatist could have elaborated so effective a plot out of the scanty materials at hand. For it must be remembered that while many an episode and speech in the play must be credited to M. Rostand's researches, its central conception must be credited to his inventive genius. This central conception is effective even if not fully great: hence it seems hardly fair to accuse him of merely writing a clever series of scenes designed to bring out the talents of a great actor. He has done this, and he has yielded to the current demand for the spectacular far more than he should have done; but, with all his errors as an artist still in his prentice days, he has developed a character and produced a moving drama. And he is surely young enough to outgrow spectacular melodrama and such opera-bouffe tricks as the introduction of a "buffet-coach" on the stage.

ROSTAND'S SKILL AS A POET

But our author is more than an effective dramatist of great promise, he is also a genuine poet. His verses lack the depth and sincerity characteristic of the poetic drama at its height in the hands of Shakespeare or Sophocles; they have not the impetus that Victor Hugo gave to his; but they possess lyric charm to a marked degree. They are never flat, though perhaps never rarely beautiful; but it is at least certain that they are the work of an opulent artist. . . .

It seems idle to deny that M. Rostand is one of the most skillful poets of our times. In view of the effectiveness of his drama, it is equally idle to deny that we have a right to look upon his play as an artistic event of international importance. For, whatever faults we may discover in *Cyrano,* we are surely somewhat blind if we do not discover in its author a remarkable affluence of power. Now affluence may be characteristic either of talents or of genius, and it would be rash to assert positively which sort of affluence M. Rostand possesses. But, after all, there are only a few affluent men born to a generation, and when the public recognizes one of them, it is surely within its rights when it greets him with acclamation. It may mistake talents, or even a single talent, for genius, but posterity can easily rectify the error, which is, at least, a generous one. Hence, those of us who have admired M. Rostand's play have no need to be ashamed to own our liking; and hence, too, any attempt, like the present translation, to make the drama better known outside of France, is to be heartily welcomed.

A Moral Hero?

Robert Metcalf Smith

Mixed in with the popular support for *Cyrano de Bergerac* was also a concern for its implications. Rostand plays on the audience's sympathy by aggrandizing Cyrano, emphasizing his panache and intelligence. However, Cyrano also woos Roxane for Christian, who wins her consent for marriage in this dishonest way. Moralists found this to be unethical conduct, unworthy of a hero. In this excerpt, Robert Metcalf Smith critiques the play in general and gives his perspective on the moral dilemma. Robert Metcalf Smith was a professor of English at Lehigh University. Smith's credits include coauthor of *Shakespeare Allusions and Parallels* and author of *Froissart and the English Chronicle Play.*

Cyrano de Bergerac is easily the outstanding romantic play of our age. First produced in Paris in 1897 (it was written while Rostand was still in his twenties) it took by storm not only France but the whole of the western world. Seldom has a drama been more extravagantly praised. Writing in the *Fortnightly Review,* soon after the first production, one critic asserted that "not even Shakespeare has given us a hero that appeals to us as Cyrano" and that there is nothing finer in "the whole range of Corneille, Racine, Molière, Victor Hugo, or any other French dramatist." It made the literary reputation of its author and of Cyrano de Bergerac as well; nor was it merely a nine days' wonder, as the success of Mr. Walter Hampden's spectacular revival in 1923 has testified. Of the plays of the romantic revival which set in at the end of the 19th century in France, *Cyrano de Bergerac* seems most likely to hold an enduring appeal for all sorts of persons both in the theater and the library.

There have been, of course, dissenting voices amid the chorus of praise. Just a few months after the enthusiastic

Excerpted from *Types of Romantic Drama,* edited by Robert Metcalf Smith (New York: Prentice-Hall, 1928).

#216 Sun Mar 02 2003 01:23PM
Item(s) checked out to p2444093.

TITLE: Jean-Jacques Rousseau and the 18t
BRCD: 06419100011943
DUE DATE: Mar 30 2003

TITLE: Cyrano de Bergerac [videorecordin
BRCD: 064103091445012
DUE DATE: Mar 09 2003

TITLE: Hobbits, elves, and wizards : exp
BRCD: 30641001512008
DUE DATE: Mar 30 2003

TITLE: Readings on Cyrano de Bergerac /
BRCD: 30641001273676
DUE DATE: Mar 30 2003

Longwood Public Library
(631) 924-6400

critic of the *Fortnightly Review,* Norman Hapgood, writing in the *Bookman,* condemned the play for its lack of sincerity, inevitability, and true greatness, while admitting its extraordinary versatility and brilliance of execution. Brander Matthews offered unfavorable criticisms, especially of the action of the drama, which he said was not true dramatic action at all but merely a constant bustle of physical activity, or stage business; and William Archer, calling it "a stirring illustration of the mendacity of useless sacrifice," pointed out that unless the "jurisdiction of rationalistic criticism were denied" the play must be condemned on the score of its false morality. The fourth act has been subjected to especially severe criticism. Meanwhile the play rides triumphantly on between the opposing camps, gaining new admirers every year.

The reasons are evident. *Cyrano de Bergerac,* possibly better than any other play . . . , combines with superb skill all the ingredients of romantic drama employed from Shakespeare's time to our own. Lively dramatic invention, splendid setting, an eloquent, witty, and adventurous hero, a conflict of passionate love with inviolable honor, joy and pathos, reckless courage and unselfish devotion, lyrical diction, and an inspiring philosophy of man's superiority to circumstance—add to these the fact that the play is avowedly a comedy, and that Cyrano's death inspires in an already admiring audience the pleasant sadness of a Viennese waltz instead of the deeper and more troubling emotions aroused by the dramas of Shakespeare, Dryden, and Stephen Phillips, and the powerful appeal of *Cyrano de Bergerac* is not difficult to understand.

UNLIKELY EVENTS

Critics who have found the extravagance of the play a source of irritation, seemingly because of their own literal-mindedness, have less ample grounds for complaint than would at first appear. There are gross improbabilities in it. Of the dozen or more which might be listed it will be sufficient to mention three or four: the fantastic balcony scene, Roxane's appearance on the battlefield, Cyrano's poetical duel with Valvert, his fight with a hundred men and, crime of crimes, a poetical pastry-cook! That these are improbabilities of the highest sort no one will deny. No one should deny them; if it be remembered that these are tricks of comic opera, that Rostand had the temerity to build an undeniably affecting romance around so unromantic a nucleus as a big nose (someone has shrewdly attributed what unity the play has to Cyrano's nose), and that Cyrano himself is a satirist of his own poetry,—in short, if it be conceded that Rostand deliberately wrote as he has written, it becomes clear that in *Cyrano de Bergerac* one has not naïve romance but sophisticated fantasy which is half satire of itself. A reading of Rostand's *The Romancers,* a satirical treatment of the Romeo and Juliet theme, or *Chantecler,* should serve to confirm this opinion.

AN EXAMINATION OF ETHICS

Here also may be found the answer to any condemnation of the play on the grounds of its false morality. There is truth in William Archer's contention that, judged prosaically, Cyrano would be reprehensible rather than commendable in his useless sacrifice. His unselfish devotion to Roxane led him into a gross deceit, which, in aiding Christian, who was unworthy, injured Roxane. Truth to himself required that he declare his love, nose or no nose. But just as we cannot condemn the play because the playwright chose to write a half satirical fantasy, so we cannot condemn it because Rostand was not an Ibsen. One cannot apply to *Cyrano de Bergerac* the logical criteria of high tragedy, for it was not written as a high tragedy, and it is manifestly unfair to demand that it be something which the author patently had no intention of making it. *Cyrano de Bergerac* takes a theme not dissimilar to that of *The Cid,* a point of honor; it humanizes that theme, charging it with an emotion that is meaningful to the playgoer of the twentieth century, and invests it with poetry and wit and a touch of satire. Cyrano's ethics may be doubtful, but he has high courage and devotion and capacity for sacrifice; to those to whom romantic drama means a confirmation of their belief in the possibilities of human nature these are not unworthy qualities.

A Timeless but Flawed Play

Max Beerbohm

In 1898, at the age of 25, Max Beerbohm had just been appointed drama critic of the *Saturday Review*, succeeding George Bernard Shaw. His review of *Cyrano de Bergerac* reflects commonly held ambivalent feelings about the play: love of the romance and dislike of the story's improbability. This doesn't prevent Beerbohm from predicting long-lasting success and affection for *Cyrano*. Max Beerbohm was a noted English essayist, critic, and caricaturist. His collected essays include *The Happy Hypocrite* and *And Even Now*. He was knighted in 1939.

July 9, 1898

The tricolour floats over the Lyceum [theater in London], and the critics are debating, with such animation as they can muster (at the fag-end of an arduous season) for a play written in a language to which they secretly prefer their own, whether *Cyrano* be a classic. Paris has declared it to be a classic, and, international courtesy apart, July is not the month for iconoclasm. And so the general tendency is to accept *Cyrano* in the spirit in which it has been offered to us. I myself go with that tendency. Even if I could, I would not whisk from the brow of M. Rostand, the talented boy-playwright, the laurels which Paris has so reverently imposed on it.

A COUNTERFEIT CLASSIC?

For even if *Cyrano* be not a classic, it is at least a wonderfully ingenious counterfeit of one, likely to deceive experts far more knowing than I am. M. Rostand is not a great original genius like (for example) M. Maeterlinck [French dramatist]. He comes to us with no marvellous revelation, but he is

Reprinted from Max Beerbohm's review of *Cyrano de Bergerac*, by Edmond Rostand, *Saturday Review*, July 9, 1898.

a gifted, adroit artist, who does with freshness and great force things that have been done before; and he is, at least, a monstrous fine fellow. His literary instinct is almost as remarkable as his instinct for the technique—the pyrotechnique—of the theatre, insomuch that I can read *Cyrano* almost as often, with almost as much pleasure, as I could see it played. Personally, I like the Byzantine manner in literature better than any other, and M. Rostand is nothing if not Byzantine: his lines are loaded and encrusted with elaborate phrases and curious conceits, which are most fascinating to anyone who, like me, cares for such things.

Yet, strange as it seems, none of these lines is amiss in the theatre. All the speeches blow in gusts of rhetoric straight over the footlights into the very lungs of the audience. Indeed, there is this unusual feature in M. Rostand's talent, that he combines with all the verbal preciosity of extreme youth the romantic ardour and technical accomplishment of middle-age. . . .

A HAND FOR DRAMA

Not the debased [French dramatist Victorien] Sardou himself has the dramaturgic touch more absolutely than has M. Rostand. But M. Rostand is not, like M. Sardou, a mere set of fingers with the theatre at the tips of them. On the contrary, he is a brain and a heart and all sorts of good things which atone for—or, rather, justify—the fact that *Cyrano* is of the stage stagey. It is rather silly to chide M. Rostand for creating a character and situations which are unreal if one examine them from a non-romantic standpoint. It is silly to insist, as one or two critics have insisted, that Cyrano was a fool and a blackguard, in that he entrapped the lady of his heart into marriage with a vapid impostor. The important and obvious point is that Cyrano, as created by M. Rostand, is a splendid hero of romance.

If you have any sensibility to romance, you admire him so immensely as to be sure that whatever he may have done was for the best. All the characters and all the incidents in the play have been devised for the glorification of Cyrano, and are but, as who should say, so many rays of lime-light converging upon him alone. And that is as it should be. The romantic play which survives the pressure of time is always that which contains some one central figure, to which everything is subordinate—a one-part play, in other words. The part of Cyrano is one which, unless I am much mistaken, the great French actor in every future generation will desire to play. Cyrano will soon crop up in opera and in ballet.

Cyrano is, in fact, as inevitably a fixture in romance as Don Quixote or Don Juan, Punch or Pierrot. Like them, he will never be out of date.

A TIMELESS PLAY

But is prophecy dangerous? Of course it is. That is the whole secret of its fascination. Besides, I have a certain amount of reason in prophesying on this point. Realistic figures perish necessarily with the generation in which they were created, and their place is taken by figures typical of the generation which supervenes. But romantic figures belong to no period, and time does not dissolve them. Already Ibsen is rather out of date—even Mr. Archer has washed his hands of Ibsen—while the elder Dumas is still thoroughly in touch with the times.

Cyrano will survive because he is practically a new type in drama. I know that the motives of self-sacrifice-in-love and of beauty-adored-by-a-grotesque are as old, and as effective, as the hills, and have been used in literature again and again. I know that self-sacrifice is the motive of most successful plays. But, so far as I know, beauty-adored-by-a-grotesque has never been used with the grotesque as stage-hero. At any rate it has never been used so finely and so tenderly as by M. Rostand, whose hideous swashbuckler with the heart of gold and the talent for improvising witty or beautiful verses—Caliban + Tartarin + Sir Galahad + Theodore Hook was the amazing recipe for his concoction—is far too novel, I think, and too convincing, and too attractive, not to be permanent.

A DEMANDING ROLE

Whether, in the meantime, Cyrano's soul has, as M. Rostand gracefully declares, passed into "vous [you], Coquelin," I am not quite sure. I should say that some of it—the comic, which is, perhaps the greater part of it—has done so. But I am afraid that the tragic part is still floating somewhere, unembodied. Perhaps the two parts will never be embodied together in the same actor.

Certainly, the comic part will never have a better billet than its first.

I have said that the play is unlikely to suffer under the lapse of time. But though it has no special place in time, in space it has its own special place. It is a work charged with its author's nationality, and only the compatriots of its author can to the full appreciate it. Much of its subtlety and beauty must necessarily be lost upon us others. To translate it into English were a terrible imposition to set any one, and not even the worst offender in literature deserves such a punishment. To adapt it were harder than all the seven labours of Hercules rolled into one, and would tax the guile and strength of even Mr. Louis Parker.

The characters in the *Chemineau* had no particular racial characteristics, and their transportation to Dorsetshire did them no harm. But there is no part of England which corresponds at all to the Midi. An adapter of *Cyrano* might lay the scene in Cornwall, call the play *Then Shall Cyrano Die?* and write in a sixth act with a chorus of fifty thousand Cornishmen bent on knowing the reason why, or he might lay it in any of the other characteristic counties of England, but I should not like to answer for the consequences. However, the play will of course be translated as it stands. And, meanwhile, no one should neglect this opportunity of seeing the original production. There is so much action in the piece, and the plot itself is so simple, and even those who know no French at all can enjoy it.

AN ELABORATE PRODUCTION

And the whole setting of the piece is most delightful. I was surprised on the first night to see how excellent was the stage management. Except for a pair of restive and absurd horses, there was no hitch, despite the difference of the Lyceum and the Porte Saint Martin. Why, by the way, are real horses allowed on the stage, where their hoofs fall with a series of dull thuds which entirely destroy illusion? Cardboard horses would be far less of a nuisance and far more convincing. However, that is a detail. I wish all my readers to see *Cyrano*. It may not be the masterpiece I think it, but at any rate it is one's money's-worth. The stalls are fifteen shillings a-piece, but there are five acts, and all the five are fairly long, and each of them is well worth three shillings. Even if one does not like the play, it will be something, hereafter, to be able to bore one's grandchildren by telling them about Coquelin as Cyrano.

CHRONOLOGY

1868

Edmond Rostand born in Marseilles on April 1.

1878

Finishes primary studies at the Thedenat School. In October, begins secondary education in Marseilles.

1884

Studies at Collège Stanislas in Paris.

1887

Wins the Marshal de Villar Prize given by the Academy of Marseilles for his essay "Two Novelists of Provence: Honoré d'Urfé and Émile Zola."

1888

Meets poet Rosemonde Gérard, niece of Marshal Gérard, at Luchon—a place he frequents for his summer vacations. Begins law studies.

1889

Le Gant Rouge (The Red Glove), a prose comedy in four acts, written in collaboration with Rosemonde's half brother, Henry Lee, is produced at Cluny Theater. The play is not successful.

1890

Publishes first collection of verse, *Les Musardises* (The Idlers); the work receives some positive criticism—Rostand is compared to nineteenth-century French poet Alfred de Musset—but sells very few copies. Marries Rosemonde Gérard on April 8.

1891

Presents *Les Deux Pierrots* (The Two Pierrots), a one-act play in verse to the Comédie Française, but it is refused. First son, Maurice, is born on May 25.

1891–1892

Works on *Alceste*, for production at Rambouillet Hôtel, but it is never finished.

1893

Les Romanesques (The Romantics), a three-act comedy in verse, is accepted by the Comédie Française.

1894

Les Romanesques debuts on May 21, with public success. Jean Rostand, future biologist, moralist, and writer, is born on October 30.

1895

The famous actor Benoît-Constant Coquelin asks Rostand to write him a play—this will be *Cyrano de Bergerac. La Princesse Lointaine* (The Faraway Princess), a play in four acts and in verse, debuts with critical success on April 5; Sarah Bernhardt, for whom Rostand wrote the play, stars in it at her Renaissance Theater.

1896

Diagnosed with neurasthenia. Takes Dreyfus's side in the Dreyfus Affair.

1897

La Samaritaine (The Woman of Samaria), an evangelical work in three tableaus, debuts on April 14; Bernhardt again stars at the Renaissance, and it is a moderate success. *Cyrano de Bergerac* debuts at the Porte-Saint-Martin Theater on December 27 and is an immediate success; it plays for four hundred performances until March 1899, and Rostand is compared to famed French author and playwright Victor Hugo; until his death in January 1909, Coquelin is the only actor to play the lead in Paris.

1898

Made a knight of the Legion of Honor. Elected to the Academy of Moral and Political Sciences. President Félix Faure attends a performance of *Cyrano* with his family on January 6.

1899

Works on *L'Aiglon* (The Eaglet) for Sarah Bernhardt.

1900

Moves to Cambo-les-Bains in the Atlantic Pyrenees because of ill health. *L'Aiglon*, a drama in six acts in verse, debuts on March 15 with Bernhardt in the role of the duke of Reichstadt; a well-attended success, but not one to equal *Cyrano*'s.

1901

Made an officer of the Legion of Honor. Elected to the French Academy on May 30; he succeeds the dramatist Henri de

Bronier, famous in his time for the triumph of *La Fille de Roland* (The Daughter of Roland), a patriotic drama in verse; Rostand's reception does not take place until June 4, 1903, because of his illness.

1904

Begins building a large house, Arnaga, near Cambo-les-Bains.

1910

Writes a fragmentary drama, *Le Bois Sacré* (The Sacred Wood), a parody of the Faust story, but it is only published posthumously. Made a commander of the Legion of Honor. Publishes *Le Cantique de l'Aile* (The Canticle of the Wing). *Chantecler* debuts at Porte-Saint-Martin on February 7 with Lucien Guitry in the lead; a large attendance does not sway the generally poor reviews.

1911

Literary activity practically ends. Writes *La Dernière Nuit de Don Juan* (The Last Night of Don Juan, first performed in 1922). Fame lives on, mainly because of innumerable revivals of *Cyrano.*

1913

Cyrano is revived at Porte-Saint-Martin Theater on March 3 and celebrates its thousandth production. (If counting productions in the provinces and in countries other than France, the number could be tripled or quadrupled.) A free public performance is given a week later as part of the celebration.

1914–1918

Refused entrance into the French army because of poor health. Writes a volume of patriotic poems, *Le Vol de la Marseillaise* (The Flight of the Marseillaise). Intensely follows the war and even visits the front in 1915. Spends the rest of his life in semi-retirement.

1918

Rostand dies on December 2 from an epidemic of the Spanish flu ravaging Paris, six weeks after the armistice.

1919

Le Vol de la Marseillaise is published.

1921

La Dernière Nuit de Don Juan is published.

1983

Cyrano de Bergerac enters the public domain.

FOR FURTHER RESEARCH

MAJOR WORKS BY EDMOND ROSTAND

Chantecler: A Play in Four Acts. Trans. Kay Nolte Smith. Lanham, MD: University Press of America, 1987.

Cyrano de Bergerac. Trans. Christopher Fry. London: Oxford University Press, 1975.

Cyrano de Bergerac. Trans. Brian Hooker. New York: Bantam Books, 1951.

Cyrano de Bergerac and Chanticleer. Trans. Clifford Hersey Bissell and William Van Wyck. Los Angeles: Ward Ritchie, 1947.

The Fantasticks: A Romantic Comedy in Three Acts. Trans. George Fleming. London: William Heinemann, 1925.

The Faraway Princess—La Princesse Lointaine: A Drama in Four Acts. Trans. John Heard Jr. New York: H. Fertig, 1987.

The Last Night of Don Juan: A Dramatic Poem. Trans. T. Lawrason Riggs. Yellow Springs, OH: Kahoe, 1930.

Plays of Edmond Rostand. Trans. Henderson Daingerfield Norman. New York: Macmillan, 1921. (Includes *The Romantics, The Princess Far Away, The Woman of Samaria, Cyrano of Bergerac, The Eaglet,* and *Chanticleer*).

The Princess Far-Away: A Romantic Tragedy in Four Acts. Trans. Anna Emilia Bagstad. Boston: R.G. Badger, 1921.

WORKS IN FRENCH

Cyrano de Bergerac. Paris: Livre de Poche, 1990.

L'Aiglon: Drame en Six Actes en Vers. Paris: Fasquelle Editeurs, 1957.

La Samaritaine: Evangile en Trois Tableaux en Vers. Paris: Librairie A. Fayard, 1941.

Les Musardises. Paris: Charpentier et Fasquelle, 1927.

Le Vol de la Marseillaise. Paris: Charpentier et Fasquelle, 1926.

Oeuvres Completes Illustrées. Paris: Lafitte, 1923. (Includes *Le Cantique de L'Aile, La Dernière Nuit de Don Juan, Chantecler, L'Aiglon, Cyrano de Bergerac, Les Musardises, Le Bois*

Sacré, Les Romanesques, La Princesse Lointaine, La Samaritaine, Le Vol de la Marseillaise, and *Les Deux Pierrots.*)

CRITICAL WORKS

Albert Bermel, ed., *The Genius of the French Theater.* New York: Mentor Books, 1961.

Frank Wadleigh Chandler, *The Contemporary Drama of France.* Boston: Little, Brown, 1920.

Helen Louise Cohen, *Milestones of the Drama.* New York: Harcourt, Brace & World, 1940.

T.S. Eliot, "Rhetoric and Poetic Drama," in *Selected Essays.* London: Faber and Faber, 1951.

Edward Freeman, *Edmond Rostand, "Cyrano de Bergerac."* Glasgow, Scotland: University of Glasgow French and German Publications, 1995.

John Gassner, ed., *A Treasury of the Theatre.* New York: Simon and Schuster, 1967.

Elliott M. Grant, ed., *Chief French Plays of the Nineteenth Century.* New York: Harper & Brothers, 1934.

Jules Lemaître, *Theatrical Impressions.* Port Washington, NY: Kennikat, 1924.

William L. Phelps, *Essays on Modern Dramatists.* Freeport, NY: Libraries, 1970.

TRANSLATIONS WITH CRITICAL INTRODUCTIONS

Edmond Rostand, *Cyrano de Bergerac.* Trans. Helen B. Dole. New York: Grosset & Dunlap, 1931.

Edmond Rostand, *Cyrano de Bergerac.* Trans. Humbert Wolfe. London: Hutchinson, 1941.

Edmond Rostand, *Cyrano de Bergerac.* Ed. Geoff Woollen. London: Bristol Classical, 1994.

Edmond Rostand, *Cyrano de Bergerac.* Ed. Oscar Kuhns. New York: H. Holt, 1899.

Edmond Rostand, *Cyrano de Bergerac.* Trans. Edwin Morgan. Manchester, England: Carcanet, 1992.

Colbert Searles, ed., *Seven French Plays.* New York: Henry Holt, 1935.

BIOGRAPHIES

Bruce Carpenter, *A Book of Dramas.* New York: Prentice-Hall, 1949. [Translation of play with author biography.]

Barrett Harper Clark, *Contemporary French Dramatists.* Cincinnati: Stewart and Kidd, 1916.

Edward Everett Hale Jr., *Dramatists of Today.* New York: H. Holt, 1911.

Microsoft Encarta 2000 Encyclopedia, "Edmond Rostand."
    Redmond, WA: Microsoft, 2000.
George Jean Nathan, *The Magic Mirror.* New York: Knopf,
    1960.
Agnes Mary Frances Robinson, *Twentieth Century French
    Writers: Reviews and Reminiscences.* Freeport, NY: Li-
    braries, 1966.

CYRANO DE BERGERAC AND RELATED HISTORY

Richard Aldington, trans., "Cyrano de Bergerac," *Voyages to
    the Moon and the Sun.* New York: E.P. Dutton, 1923.
Erica Harth, *"Cyrano de Bergerac" and the Polemics of
    Modernity.* New York: Columbia University Press, 1970.
Wolfgang Leiner, ed., *Seventeenth Century French Literature
    at the MLA, 1985–1986: And Other Contributions on Bour-
    sault, Corneille, Cyrano, Durand, La Fontaine, Moliére.*
    Seattle: Papers on French Seventeenth Century Literature,
    1987.

INDEX